CRETE

Text: Dora Konsola

Translation: Alexandra Doumas

Photographs: I. Dekopoulos

Printing: I. Dekopoulos

Phototyping: FOTOMCA

Dora Konsola
Archaeologist

CRETE

KNOSSOS–PHAISTOS–AGHIA TRIADA GORTYN–MALIA–ZAKROS–GOURNIA HERAKLEION MUSEUM

Aghios Nikolaos Museum — Chania Museum

JOHN DECOPOULOS
6 APOLLONOS STR. HELLINICO - ATHENS
TEL. 99.13.790 - 99.22.699
©

Athens 1983

Table of Contents:

Foreword:

The main aim of this guidebook is to give the reader as complete a picture as possible of the important archaeological sites and museums of Crete.

The description of the sites is quite analytical, with information on the latest scholarly opinions, yet not overburdened with tedious details and technical terms. After a brief introduction to the location of the sites, their excavation and importance, there follows a tour of each, accompanied by a plan, to facilitate clearer understanding of the topography.

At the beginning of the book there is a brief but informative review of the history of ancient Crete. Of the archaeological sites the palace of Knossos is described first, in considerable detail, for it is the most important. There follows a tour of the galleries of the Herakleion Archaeological Museum which should always be combined with the visit to Knossos. The palace of Phaistos, villa of Aghia Triada and Gortyn, which are described next, are usually included in a one-day excursion to south-central Crete. Next comes a description of the palace of Malia which is on the road towards eastern Crete, where the palace of Zakros is located, as well as the settlement of Gournia. The guidebook ends with a brief mention of the archaeological museums of Aghios Nikolaos, Rethymnon and Chania.

Dora Konsola

Brief historical outline of ancient Crete

Man first appeared on Crete during the 7th millennium BC, at the beginning of the **Neolithic era,** as far as we know to date. Throughout the whole of this period Crete was somewhat isolated and did not follow the cultural developments taking place on the Greek mainland.

In around 2600 BC, or slightly earlier, fundamental changes took place with the introduction of the first metal, bronze, and the appearance of new ethnic elements originating from at least two different regions, Asia Minor and Libya. During this period the Minoan civilisation started taking shape. Its first phase is known as the **Prepalatial** (2600-1900 BC), since there were not yet kings or palaces. Seafaring was in the ascendancy as well as trade and the first significant works of art were created, especially in the fields of stoneworking, jewellery, sealstone carving and pottery.

The first palaces were built in about 1900 BC at key points on the island (Knossos, Phaistos, Malia, Zakros) and the **Protopalatial** period (1900-1700 BC) commenced. All offices were concentrated in the hands of the king who systematically organised the administration, trade and production, even the religion of Crete. With its mighty navy, Crete dominated the entire Aegean. At this time Hieroglyphic script, the oldest form of writing in Crete, was disseminated. Of the arts, pottery, in particular, flourished with the famous polychrome Kamares vases. This important period terminates with the destruction of the palaces, possibly by earthquakes, in 1700 BC.

Immediately afterwards, on the same sites, new luxurious palaces were built and the Minoan civilisation entered its most splendid phase, the **Neopalatial** (1700-1400 BC). Its influence radiated throughout virtually the whole of the Eastern Mediterranean. Relations between the different kingdoms of the island were pacific, as is evident from the absence of fortifications around the palaces and towns. Art achieved its zenith and masterpieces were created in the spheres of wall-painting, sculpture, pottery, sealstone carving, metalwork, goldsmithing. There were developments too in the field of writing, with the simplification and schematisation of the hieroglyphic signs to create the script known as Linear A. Around 1450 BC there was a sudden destruction of the Minoan centres. According to the well-known theory of Spyridon Marinatos, this destruction was due to the terrific eruption of the Thera volcano which generated enormous tidal waves and earthquakes. Only Knossos was not totally obliterated. There followed an invasion by Achaeans-Mycenaeans from the Greek mainland, who installed their own dynasty in the palace of Knossos. However, recently, many scholars have maintained that this eruption occured earlier (1500 BC) and only caused minimal damage to Crete and that the final destruction came with the incursion of the Mycenaeans in 1450 BC. The Mycenaeans introduced new elements into the way of life and art. A new script evolved at this time, Linear B, a modified version of Linear A (period of Mycenaean domination at Knossos 1450-1380 BC). In about 1380 BC Knossos was finally destroyed by a cause unknown, and the **Postpalatial** period (1380 - 1110 BC) began. Large palaces no longer existed and Crete ceased to play an important role in the Aegean. The old Minoan tradition continued but was decisively influenced by the Mycenaean civilisation of Mainland Greece. In art there appeared a formalisation and stylisation which, as time elapsed, led to decline.

Meanwhile, one of the new Hellenic tribes had reached the island and begun to settle there, the warlike Dorians. Their advent heralded a change in the structure of society and a new era was initiated for Crete, different from the preceding ones. Also at this time iron first appeared, replacing bronze. In the first two centuries (**Subminoan** and **Protogeometric** period 1100 - 900 BC) the decline and fall was total. However, in the following periods (**Geometric** 900 - 725 BC and **Orientalising** 725 - 650 BC), when prevailing circumstances were more favourable, significant examples of pottery and metalworking were produced. By the next period, the **Archaic** (650 - 500 BC) mighty city-states were already in existence (Knossos, Phaistos, Lyttos, Axos, Aptera, Kydonia et al.) in which the body politic and way of life were organised in accordance with the Spartan model. The system of government was oligarchic and conservative and the education of each citizen militaristic in character. In this same era wonderful early works of monumental sculpture, the so-called «Daedalic», were created.

In **Classical** (500 - 330 BC) and **Hellenistic** (330 - 67 BC) times Crete did not participate in the major historical events of the rest of Greece. The island's history was restricted to continual internecine rivalries between the different cities. Creativity in the artistic field was somewhat impoverished. Later (69 BC) the Romans took the opportunity of interfering and after two years of harsh protracted hostilities they subjugated the island. It became a Roman province with its capital at Gortyn on the Mesara plain. Throughout this era, known as the **GrecoRoman** (67 BC - 323 AD) conditions were favourable to the development of art and, in particular, sculpture.

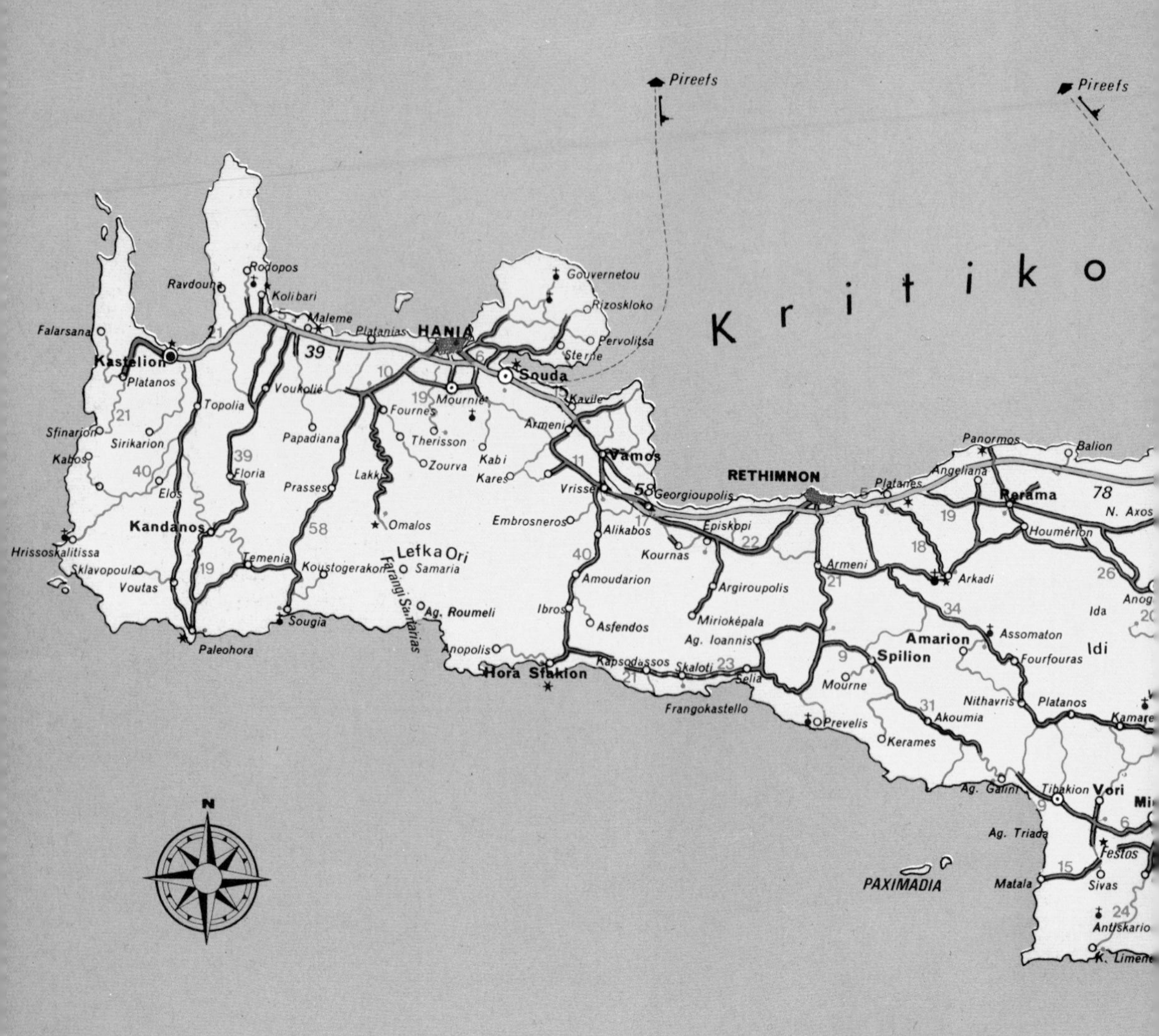

Pireefs
Pireefs
K r i t i k o
Rodopos
Ravdouha
Kolibari
Maleme
Falarsana
Kastelion
Platanos
Topolia
Voukolié
Platanias
HANIA
Souda
Gouvernetou
Rizoskloko
Pervolitsa
Sterne
Fournes
Mournié
Therisson
Armeni
Kabi
Kares
Zourva
Vamos
Vrisses
Papadiana
Prasses
Lakki
Omalos
Sfinarion
Sirikarion
Kabos
Elos
Floria
Kandanos
Hrissoskalitissa
Sklavopoula
Voutas
Temenia
Koustogerakon
Samaria
Lefka Ori
Farangi Samarias
Ag. Roumeli
Sougia
Paleohora
Anopolis
Hora Sfakion
Embrosneros
Alikabos
Amoudarion
Ibros
Asfendos
Kapsodassos
Skaloti
Selia
Frangokastello
Georgioupolis
RETHIMNON
Episkopi
Kournas
Argiroupolis
Mirioképala
Ag. Ioannis
Armeni
Mourne
Spilion
Amarion
Prevelis
Kerames
Akoumia
Nithavris
Platanos
Fourfouras
Assomaton
Arkadi
Houmérion
Perama
N. Axos
Panormos
Balion
Angeliana
Platanes
Ida
Idi
Ag. Galini
Tibakion
Vori
Ag. Triada
Festos
Matala
Sivas
PAXIMADIA
N

AFRICA Libya U. A. R.

THE PALACE OF KNOSSOS

The palace of Knossos is also known as the palace of Minos, since Knossos is associated in mythology with Minos, son of Zeus and Europe, who was king of Knossos and a famous judge and legislator.

It is the largest of the four palaces to have been excavated so far on Crete. It covers an area of 22,000 sq. m. and is several storeys high.

Its discovery is the achievement of the great English archaeologist Arthur Evans, who worked with deep scholarly knowledge and indefatigable enthusiasm to bring to light the most perfect and impressive creation of Minoan architecture. Excavations at Knossos commenced in 1900 and within four years (till 1903) virtually the whole of the palace had been revealed. Investigation in the surrounding region continued, with interruptions, until 1931. During this interval extraordinary works of art were uncovered, astonishing the whole world. Statuettes of precious materials, outstanding stone ritual vessels, splendid polychrome wall-paintings and other objects which one may admire in the galleries of the Herakleion Museum. These finds and the excavation in general are presented in an exemplary manner in Evans' famous four-volume work «The Palace of Minos at Knossos» (1921 - 1935).

Nowadays, the enormous multi-storeyed palace, after Evans' extensive and somewhat audacious reconstructions, (in which he used a great deal of cement, a material foreign to Minoan architecture) gives the visitor a wonderful idea of the architecture and life in general in Minoan times. To visit it is an unforgettable experience. It consists of hundreds of rooms, daedalic corridors, porticoes, courts, staircases etc. At first glance the overall impression is chaotic and brings to mind the mythical labyrinth, the maze-like lair of the Minotaur. Indeed, it seems that the ruins of the palace with their complex design, were the real reason for the evolution of the myth of the labyrinth*. However, on more careful inspection one is soon convinced that the huge building is not the result of chance development, but was conceived of and designed with attention right from the beginning in order to accomodate the diverse functions focussed on the palace. For the Cretan palaces differed from those of later times. The palace was not simply the residence of the royal family but constituted the centre of political, economic and religious life of each region. Thus, in separate sectors were the luxurious royal apartments and formal reception halls, in another sector the important chambers for the cult of the deity and major religious festivals, in others the rows of magazines in which produce was stored not only for the needs of the royal family but also for trading transactions, and in another sector the workshops in which precious works of art were manufactured.

The history of the site goes back to Neolithic times when there was a large and significant settlement at Knossos. Occupation also continued throughout the Prepalatial period, as is evident from the few traces which

* The word **labyrinth** is derived from the prehellenic word Labrys: double axe and seems to have meant the House of the Double Axe. This may have been the name of the palace of Knossos, on the walls and pillars of which this sacred symbol is inscribed several times.

have been found here. In about 1900 BC the first palace was built on top of the hill and existed until 1700 BC, when it was destroyed by earthquake. Immediately afterwards a new palace was founded on the same site. This too suffered serious damage in 1450 BC when the rest of the palaces were completely destroyed. There followed the invasion of the Achaeans-Mycenaeans who captured the palace and installed their own dynasty. Mycenaean domination lasted until 1380 BC when the palace was finally destroyed and ceased to be the seat of the king. Later, in the Postpalatial period, certain parts were temporarily repaired and it was inhabited by private individuals («Reoccupation period»).

Around the magnificent palace a large city grew up, the population of which is estimated to have been 30,000. A few houses of this city have been excavated and, in the main, large buildings in the vicinity of the palace which must have been connected with it (the Royal Villa to the NE, the Little Palace to the NW, the Caravanserai (hospice) to the south). The city was surrounded by its cemeteries (Isopata, Aghios Ioannis, Zapher Papoura, Sanatorio, Gypsades, Profitis Elias) from which interesting finds have been recovered. The city of Knossos is about 4 km. inland from the north shore, yet it had two large harbours. One was at present-day Katsambas on the estuary of the Kairatos river and the other at Amnissos, east of Herakleion.

Before beginning our visit, we should bear in mind that the nucleus of

Palace of Knossos. Reconstruction of the facade of the west wing, overlooking the central court (after Evans).

the palace is the large Central Court and the building complex is basically divided into two wings: the West Wing, in which are the shrines and magazines and the East Wing, in which are the apartments of the royal family and the artisans' workshops. There were entrances on all sides but the most important was the west one, through which we enter the palace today.

West Wing:

First we encounter the large paved **West Court.** It is traversed by pathways, raised above the level of the rest of the paving, which were used for the passage of holy processions on major festival days («Processional Causeways»). In the large circular pits **Kouloures,** which we see to the left, broken vessels used for offerings made in the palace shrines were thrown (sacral deposits). The remnants of two built **altars** at two points in the court constitute yet further proof that religious ceremonies took place in this space. In front of us is the magnificent West Front of the palace. The blackened massive stone blocks in the lower courses clearly display traces of the terrible fire which destroyed the palace in its final phase.

One of the processional causeways of the court leads to a **propylon** with single column (the base is preserved) through which one reaches the interior of the palace. The two rooms on the right would have been for the porter and for the official who controlled the entrance. The long corridor with polychrome paving slabs, known as the **Corridor of the Procession,** on account of the large mural on its walls, commences here. The wall-painting depicted a procession of youths carrying ritual vases. The south part of the corridor has been destroyed which is why, nowadays, we turn eastwards before reaching its end, and are confronted by the **South Propylaia,** which was the official entrance. To north and south of the central gateway is a two-columned portico. In the restored west section of the Propylaia there is a copy of the wall-painting of the procession, which would have continued as far as here. The large poros-stone horns of consecration (much restored), which have been set up on the right, embellished one of the windows of the palace. The horns of consecration (horns of the holy animal, the bull) were an important religious symbol in Minoan times and quite often stone replicas of these were set up on top of the facades of palaces and shrines.

On the south side of the palace, at a lower level, we see from above the remains of the **South House,** which must have been the residence of the Chief Priest, and the **South Entrance** of the palace, which was a simple structure and in all likelihood a service entrance.

A wide **flight of steps** leads from the propylaia to the **upper storey,** known as the Piano nobile, an Italian term used to describe the upper floor of Renaissance palaces. The floor of this storey has been reconstructed, as have several column bases in various rooms which seem to have been used for cult purposes: the «Tricolumnar Shrine» and its Treasury with wonderful stone ritual vessels, the «Great Hall» and the «Hall of the Shrine».

Looking westwards from the first floor we see, on the ground floor, the long **Corridor of the Magazines** which divides the West Wing from N to S.

Along the length of the west side there is a series of long narrow magazines, in many of which the enormous pithoi (storage jars) which contained oil and wine are still «in situ». In the rectangular cists beneath the floor of the magazines precious objects were concealed. It seems that these magazines had a holy character and within them were accumulated large quantities of agricultural produce which were offerings from citizens to the deity and the king, who ruled as her divine representative on earth.

A staircase at the north edge of the terrace leads down to the ground floor from where we begin our visit to the religious apartments which occupied the major part of the east side of the West Wing. First we enter the **Lobby** of the Throne Room in the middle of which there is a large porphyry basin, perhaps for purification and sprinkling. On the wall to left and right there are benches, flanking a wooden throne which is a copy of the stone

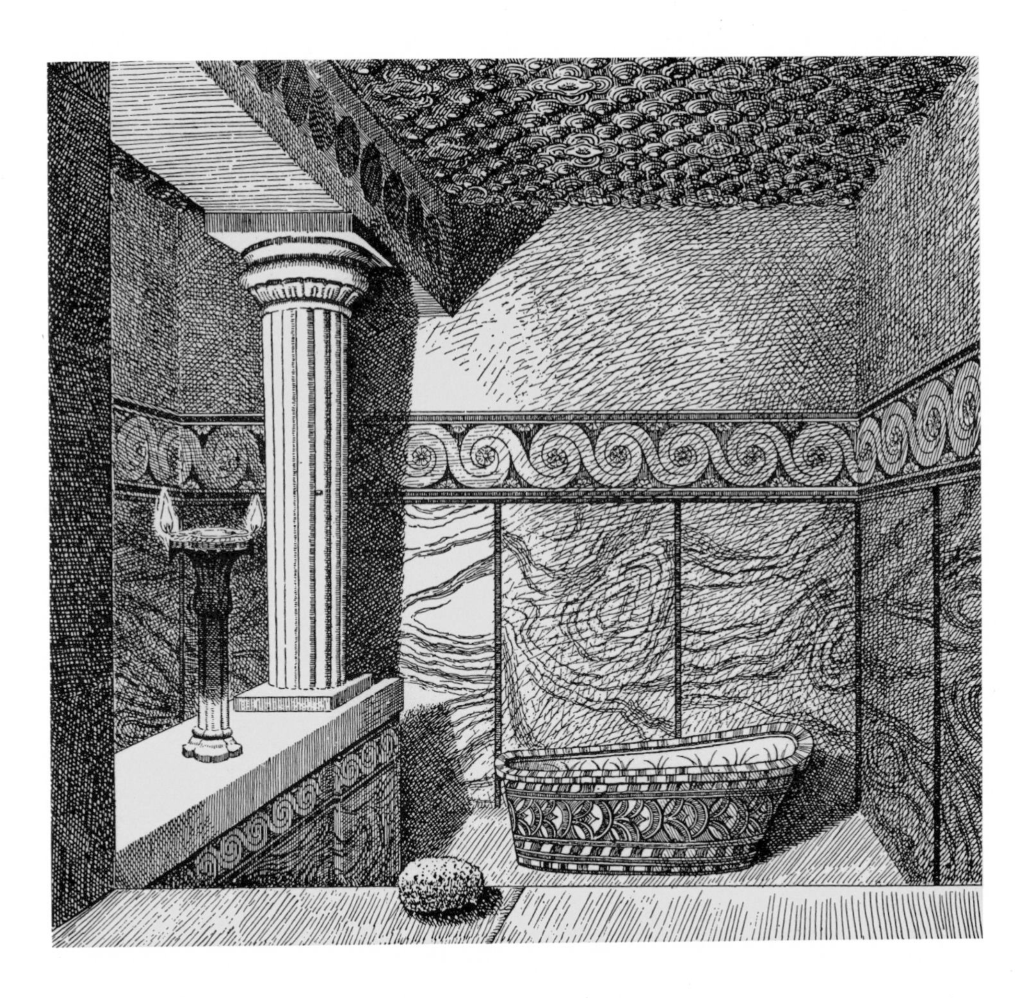

Palace of Knossos. Reconstruction of the bathroom in the Quee's Apartment (after Evans).

one in the next room. The famous **Throne Room** was perhaps the most formal area for religious ceremonies in the palace. Here, in the centre of the north wall, stands the magnificent alabaster «Throne of Minos» which has been preserved intact and is considered to be the oldest throne in Europe. It has a high back with undulating outline and, from its details, seems to have copied a wooden prototype. Painted on the wall on either side of the throne are wingless griffins, mythical beasts with lion's body, eagle's head and serpent's tail, a much loved theme in Cretomycenaean art, which must have had especial symbolic significance. Next to the throne there are benches, probably for the priests, and opposite, at a lower level, a **Lustral Basin** in which purification and sprinkling with holy water took place. All the evidence suggests that this hall had a religious character and that the king or queen sat on the throne while performing official priestly duties. On the paved floor near the throne some alabaster vessels were found which had evidently been used in the final holy rite and hastily abandoned by the priests when they fled just before the palace was destroyed. It should be noted here that this arrangement of the Throne Room dates from the era of the Mycenaean hegemony at the palace of Knossos.

We now pass into the **Central Court** of the palace. It is a large open space of dimensions 50 × 30 metres, and unites the wings of the palace. On the occasion of large religious festivals a sizeable crowd could gather here. Next to the Lobby of the Throne Room there is a wide **staircase,** with column bases down the middle, which led to the upper floor. Next we come to the columned facade of the **Tripartite Shrine,** and behind it, the **Temple Repositories** wherein various ritual vessels, symbols and figurines of precious materials were uncovered inside large rectangular cists. Among these objects were the famous «Snake Goddesses» faience figurines depicting female deities, perhaps mother and daughter, with snakes (symbol of the chthonic world) in their hands. Next to the Temple Repositories there is a spacious paved lobby with benches and to the west of this are the dark, mysterious **Pillar Crypts.** In the middle of both crypts there is a rectangular pillar on which the sacred symbol of the double axe has been carved several times. The shallow grooves around their bases were to receive the blood from sacrifices or libations. Pillars were certainly regarded as holy in Minoan times and rituals must have been performed within the crypts, though it is impossible to know details of these nowadays.

On the upper storeys of the south sector of the West Wing there were porticoes and verandahs from where the nobles could watch the festivities in the Central Court. A little further down, on the east wall of the corridor leading from the south to the Central Court, a copy of the relief fresco of the **Prince with the Lilies** has been placed. It depicts a king or prince-priest wearing a magnificent crown with lilies and peacock plumes and a necklace of lily-shaped beads. One arm is extended behind and was pulling the lead of an animal which has not survived, perhaps a griffin or a sphinx.

East Wing

We now cross the Central Court in the direction of the East Wing which was probably 4 or 5 storeys high. Two or three storeys were above the level of the court, while the others were constructed at a level deeper than that of the Central Court, for which reason a large vertical cutting had been made in the east side of the hill. The East Wing housed the private apartments of the royal family, the seat of political authority, the royal workshops and magazines. The **staircase** which permitted communication between the floors is regarded as one of the outstanding achievements of Minoan architecture. It has broad, shallow treads of gypsum and was lit by a large lightwell surrounded by columns. As we descend it we come to the so-called **Terrace of the Royal Guard,** a verandah on which there are copies of wall-paintings depicting the characteristic figure-of-eight shields. Perhaps it was here that the guards who controlled the entrance to the royal quarters were posted. We go down a further flight and reach the very bottom of the staircase and the **King's Megaron.** First we enter the **Hall of the Double Axes** which was named after the symbol of the double axe incised on the walls of the lightwell to the west of it. Perhaps it was here that the king received official visitors since, on the north wall, there was a throne with wooden canopy, as is evident from the imprints upon the mass of lime plaster which covered it after the destruction of the palace. The hall adjacent is the **King's Megaron** proper. Here we see one of the

Palace of Knossos. Reconstruction of the Throne Room (after Evans).

characteristic apartments of Minoan architecture. The hall has a pier-and-door partition (polythyron), that is several openings on three of its walls which were closed with wooden doors. When the doors were open and the flaps folded against the recesses in the jambs, the room looked as if there were no walls around, just columns. So the royal family were assured of a pleasant sojourn during the warm summer months for the rooms were filled with light and air. When the doors remained closed, the hall was isolated from the adjacent rooms. On the two exteriors of the polythyron there are porticoes and a court.

A dark, narrow corridor leads from the Hall of the Double Axes to the **Queen's Megaron,** which is smaller and somewhat isolated. The room in which we are standing has a portico and lightwell on its two sides. Its main wall was decorated with the delightful mural of the blue dolphins, a copy of which can be seen. Another copy of a wall-painting, depicting a twirling dancing girl, has been placed on the jamb of one of the large windows overlooking the eastern portico. The small room to the west is thought to have been a **bathroom,** since close to the entrance a clay bathtub was found which has been placed inside it nowadays. However, it may have been a bedchamber. It seems that the main bedrooms must have been on the floor just above, which was similarly arranged. Another narrow corridor leads to the Queen's **Toilet** which has a low bench for toiletry vessels, a lavatory with running water, which must have had a wooden seat in those days and a small court which is, at the same time, a lightwell. It is known as the **Court of the Distaffs** since this symbol has been scratched on its walls.

For those wishing to see the south sector of the east side, it is worth pausing at the small room which has been named the **Shrine of the Double Axes.** It is a shrine of the Postpalatial period in which characteristic finds were uncovered. Standing on a pebbled base were models of sacral horns, a miniature double axe and clay figurines of worshippers and a deity with arms raised in an attitude of blessing or epiphany. Slightly further down there is yet another **Lustral Basin.**

Beyond the southeast limit of the palace we see various **private houses** which have been named: House of the Sacrificed Oxen, House of the Fallen Blocks, House of the Chancel Screen and Southeast House.

We now retrace our steps and turn northwards in order to take a look at the workshops and magazines occupying the north sector of the East Wing. From the corridor which divides this wing into two and which is at a lower level, we turn left and arrive at the **Lapidaries' Workshop.** The blocks of Spartan basalt which are still in position indicate that here was a workshop for the manufacture of stone vases. Next to it is a room with benches and shallow troughs which is considered to have been a **potter's workshop** where the clay was prepared. We cross the court, noticing the traces of the ancient drainage system, and reach the staircase, which leads eastwards, and opposite us are the large magazines. These are the **Magazines of the Giant Pithoi** which belonged to the first palace. The giant pithoi or storage jars are embellished with numerous handles and relief decoration imitating the ropes with which they were bound. We descend the stairway and arrive at the **East Bastion,** a tower-like structure from where steps lead to the outside of the palace and the verdant banks of the Kairatos river. Along the entire length of this flight of steps there is an impressive, indeed ingenious, system of lateral conduits describing a series of parabolic curves, to check the force of the water, and small settling tanks at intervals for deposition of sediment. We mount this staircase yet again, pass by the Magazines of the Giant Pithoi, and higher up, on the left we enter a long corridor known as the **Corridor of the Draughtboard.** It was so named because a royal gaming board (something like chess or backgammon), made of precious materials, was found here. Underneath the floor of this corridor the clay pipes of the palace plumbing system can be seen. Beyond the southern end of the corridor there is an area where traces of the drainage system can be seen. It is considered to have been the most advanced system in antiquity, unrivalled until Roman times. Adjacent is the **Magazine of the Medallion Pithoi** in which the large pithoi decorated with relief medallions are still «in situ». Above this magazine and above the rooms to east and west of it was a spacious formal chamber with an internal peristyle (the East Hall). This hall has not been preserved, but from fragments of wall-paintings which had fallen into the ground floor (griffins leashed to columns, athletes) it may be inferred that it was splendidly decorated. Perhaps it was the Throne Room proper, the seat of the king's political authority.

North Wing

Once again we come out into the Central Court of the palace and proceed northwards. In the northwest wing of the palace a complex of holy rooms was revealed in which there were the well-known miniature frescoes depicting religious gatherings and the Saffron Gatherer fresco depicting a blue monkey picking crocuses. Many clay tablets in Linear B script were found in one room which must have been part of the palace archive during the period of Mycenaean domination. This complex was built on top of six very deep, narrow rooms without openings, dated to Protopalatial times. Evans called them **dungeons,** though they were most probably grain silos.

We now enter the **Corridor of the North Entrance** which is arranged in a particularly magnificent manner. The corridor is narrow and slopes downwards. It was protected by two tall bastions with colonnades to right and left. The West bastion has been restored and on the wall of its portico hangs a copy of the famous relief wall-painting of the bellowing bull. The scene perhaps showed the capture of a wild bull which would later have participated in the bull sports. We proceed to the north end of the corridor and enter the large hall with eight pillars and two columns which Evans named the **Customs House.** Perhaps it was used for the temporary storage of merchandise brought from the harbour of Knossos, since here is the terminus of the road from there. Above this hall, on the upper storey, was a similar room with two rows of internal supports, probably the palace Banqueting Hall.

We come out of the gateway on the west side of the Customs House and visit the **North Lustral Basin** which has been restored. A staircase, with

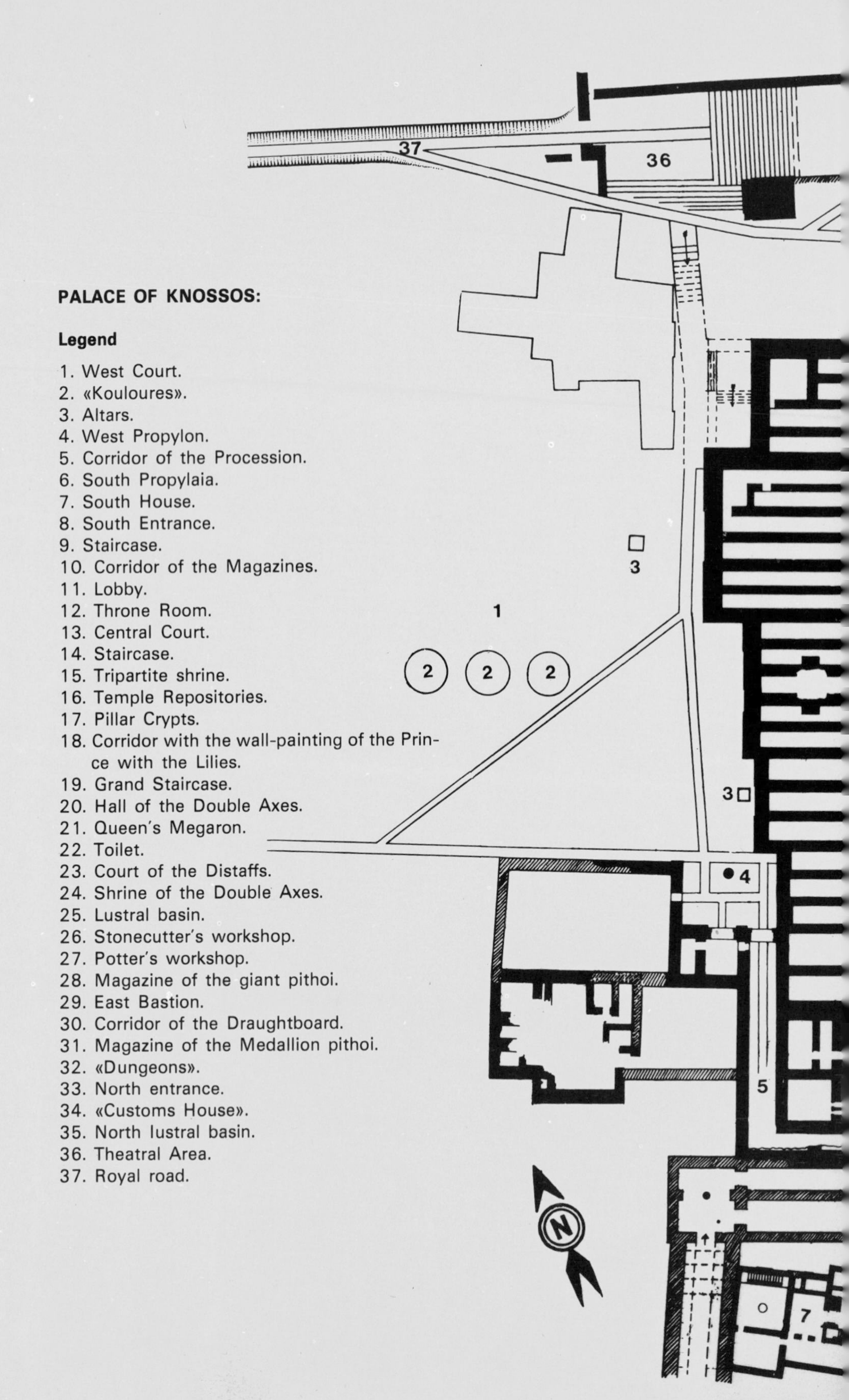

PALACE OF KNOSSOS:

Legend

1. West Court.
2. «Kouloures».
3. Altars.
4. West Propylon.
5. Corridor of the Procession.
6. South Propylaia.
7. South House.
8. South Entrance.
9. Staircase.
10. Corridor of the Magazines.
11. Lobby.
12. Throne Room.
13. Central Court.
14. Staircase.
15. Tripartite shrine.
16. Temple Repositories.
17. Pillar Crypts.
18. Corridor with the wall-painting of the Prince with the Lilies.
19. Grand Staircase.
20. Hall of the Double Axes.
21. Queen's Megaron.
22. Toilet.
23. Court of the Distaffs.
24. Shrine of the Double Axes.
25. Lustral basin.
26. Stonecutter's workshop.
27. Potter's workshop.
28. Magazine of the giant pithoi.
29. East Bastion.
30. Corridor of the Draughtboard.
31. Magazine of the Medallion pithoi.
32. «Dungeons».
33. North entrance.
34. «Customs House».
35. North lustral basin.
36. Theatral Area.
37. Royal road.

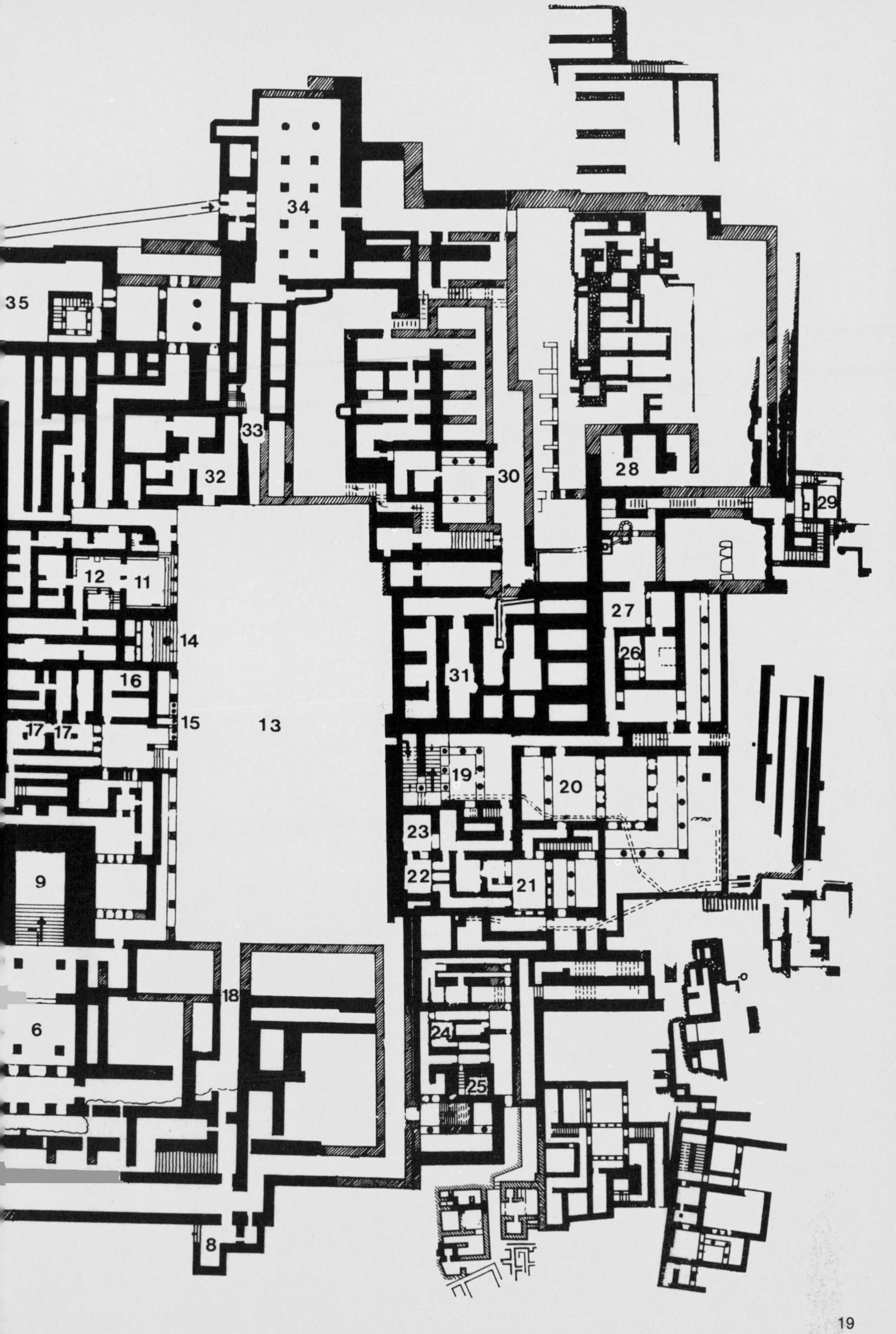
34
35
33
32
30
28
29
12
11
14
31
27
26
16
15
13
17
17
19
20
9
23
22
21
18
6
24
25
8

columns along one side, leads down into the basin with its gypsum-faced walls and frescoes. Evans thought that the precinct around the lustral basin was an «initiation area» and that the initiates first entered the lustral basin for religious purification and sprinkling and then went into the west sector of the palace.

The final area we come to, as we proceed towards the West Court, whence we commenced our visit to the palace, is the **Theatre.** It consists of two flights of steps in tiers which meet at a right angle, a tower-like building in the corner and a paved space in front of them. It is presumed that the steps were seats for the audience and the tower-like building a box for the royal family. It is estimated that about 500 spectators could watch the ritual performances which would have been presented in the paved space. However, other scholars believe that it was here that the king would have received official guests or sat in judgement upon important cases. A road leads off from the paved space and continues westwards, passing between rich houses (the «Arsenal», the «House of the Frescoes»), finally terminating at the Little Palace, a luxurious building within which the famous steatite rhyton of the bull's head was found. This road is paved and has a double row of rectangular flags down the middle along which religious processions and dignitaries would have passed. It is called the **Royal Road** and is considered to be the oldest road in Europe.

View of the Central Court and the West Wing from NE.

Palace of Knossos. General view.

Copy of part of the wall-painting of the «Gift bearers», from the South Propylaia.

The restored sector of the South Propylaia.

The restored part of the South Propylaia and huge stone sacral horns.

Colonnade of the lightwell of the staircase of the East Wing.

The «Prince with the Lilies» or «Priest-King». Relief wall-painting.

Upper part of the lightwell of the Throne Room with copies of wall-paintings from various rooms of the palace.

The «Throne Room» with the alabaster throne and copy of the wall-painting of griffins.

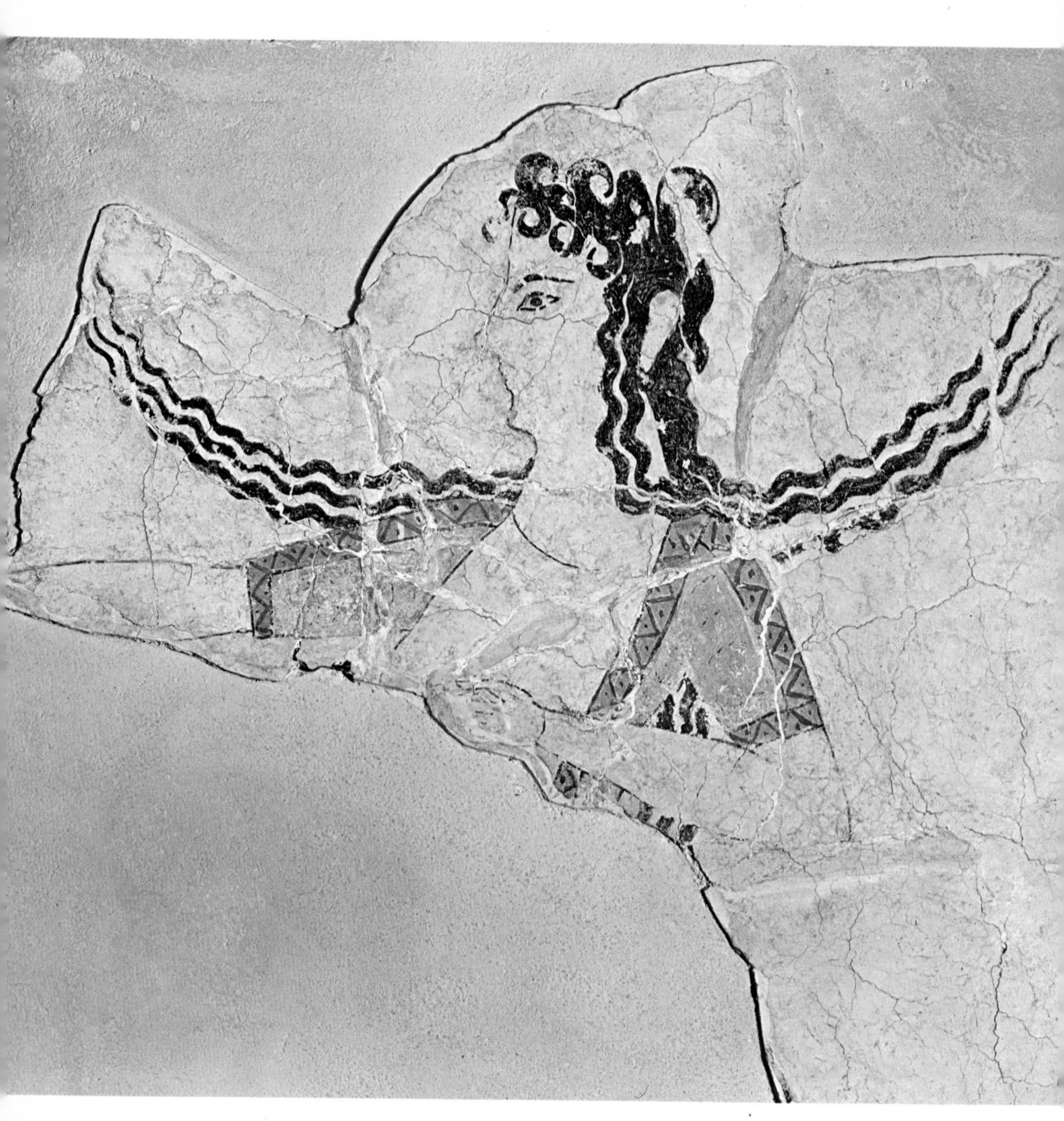

The «Dancing girl». Wall-painting from the palace of Knossos.

The «Queen's Megaron» with copy of the wall-painting of the blue dolphins.

The «Terrace of the Royal Guard» with the wall-painting of the figure-of-eight shields, in the East Wing.

The restored West Bastion of the North Entrance. ↑ →

Part of the portico of the West Bastion of the North Entrance with copy of the bull wall-painting.

Magazine of the West Wing with enormours pithoi and cists beneath the floor.

Pithos from the «magazine of the tall pithoi», in the west wing.

HERAKLEION ARCHAEOLOGICAL MUSEUM

This is one of the largest and most important museums in Greece and unique in the world for the study of the Minoan civilisation. Exhibited in its twenty galleries (I-XX) are objects representative of the developmental phases of the civilisation of Crete from Neolithic times until the Roman era.

The objects are displayed, basically, in chronological order. In the first gallery there are finds of the Neolithic and Prepalatial period. Galleries II - X follow, in which there are representative finds of the Protopalatial, Neopalatial and Postpalatial civilisation and then galleries XI and XII with objects of Early and Late Geometric and Orientalising periods. In the large ground floor vestibule, from which there is access to the upper storey, Minoan sarcophagi are displayed. In the large and two smaller rooms above, Minoan wall-paintings are exhibited. A further two rooms of the upper storey contain the Yamalakis Gollection and small finds of the Greek and Roman era, respectively. The last two galleries of the museum (XIX and XX), on the east side of the ground floor, are given over to Archaic, Classical and Hellenistic sculpture.

The most important galleries are I, III, IV, VII, VIII and XIV. Prior to one's visit it is worthwhile reading the introduction to the present guide in order to familiarise oneself with the characteristics of each period in Crete's history.

GALLERY I

Finds of the **Neolithic** period and many noteworthy examples of the art of the **Prepalatial period** (2600 - 1900 BC) which is the first phase of the Minoan civilisation.

Cases 1 & 2

Representative finds of the Neolithic era in Crete, the majority from the Neolithic settlement underneath the palace of Knossos. Handmade vases (without the use of the potter's wheel) with simple forms and dark monochrome surface. A few are decorated with incisions and dots. Figurines, mostly female. A male marble figurine (case 2) is outstanding. Stone weapons and bone tools.

Case 3

Prepalatial pottery, mainly representing two pottery styles. Pyrgos style: tall chalices with simple linear decoration made by burnishing their dark surface. It seems that they imitate wooden vessels. Also double and triple cups (kernoi) which were used for the offering of liquids and fruits to the deity. Aghios Onouphrios style: ewers and cups with clusters of dense lines in red on the light-coloured ground of the vase.

Case 6

Impressive Prepalatial Vasiliki style vases. Beak-spouted ewers and long-spouted «teapots», their surfaces covered with decorative spots caused by uneven firing.

Case 7

Wonderful stone vases from graves on the island of Mochlos in East Crete. The variety and elegance of forms is impressive, as is the skillful adaptation to the natural veins or spots of the multicoloured stones. Of interest is the green steatite pyxis, the handle of which is in the form of a reclining dog.

Case 10

Polychrome pottery from the settlement of Palaikastro. Also of interest: model of a boat with high prow and low stern, votive cups with moulded animals on the inside, votive basin with moulded herd of animals and shepherd and clay four-wheeled cart, the oldest cart model in Europe.

Case 11

Prepalatial seals which were used for sealing boxes, vases etc. They are made of soft materials (steatite or ivory) and exhibit a considerable diversity of shapes. Mainly abstract decorative designs and animals are depicted on their sealing surfaces and, very occasionally, human figures. Outstanding is a seal in the form of a seated monkey, one in the shape of a dove and another in the shape of a fly. A large seal from Archanes is in the form of three cubes, so arranged that the seal has 13 sealing surfaces each showing a different subject.

Case 12

Vases from the tholos tombs of Mesara. Charming libation vase in the form of a bull with human figures clambering over its horns, primitive representation of «bull-leaping». The large double-nozzled funnel was used for filling a double vase.

Case 13

Marble, stone and ivory figurines, the majority female. Some with pointed chin and pointed lower part are of Libyan provenance. Others, with hands folded across the chest, are of the characteristic Cycladic type.

Case 14

Bronze, and some luxurious silver, daggers. Also bronze tools and tweezers.

Case 15

On the bottom shelf, interesting stone vases from the tholos tombs of Mesara. Nest-shaped vases predominate, as well as double, triple and quadruple «kernoi» for funerary offerings.

Case 17

Wonderful jewellery of exquisite workmanship from tombs of Mochlos and Mesara. There are fine gold-leaf diadems, bands for binding the eyes of the dead, adornments for the head in the form of flowers and leaves, pendants for the neck hanging from fine chains et al. Outstanding: small frog with granular decoration on the back, votive breast, cylindrical bead with filigree decoration et al. Also very beautiful are necklaces of different coloured semiprecious stones, such as rock crystal, red sard, purple amethyst et al.

Case 18A

Finds from the Prepalatial tholos tomb at Archanes. Cycladic figurines including a unique one of ivory.

Stone vase from the islet of Mochlos.

Clay Vasiliki style ew

Ivory seal.

Jewellery of gold and semiprecious stones.

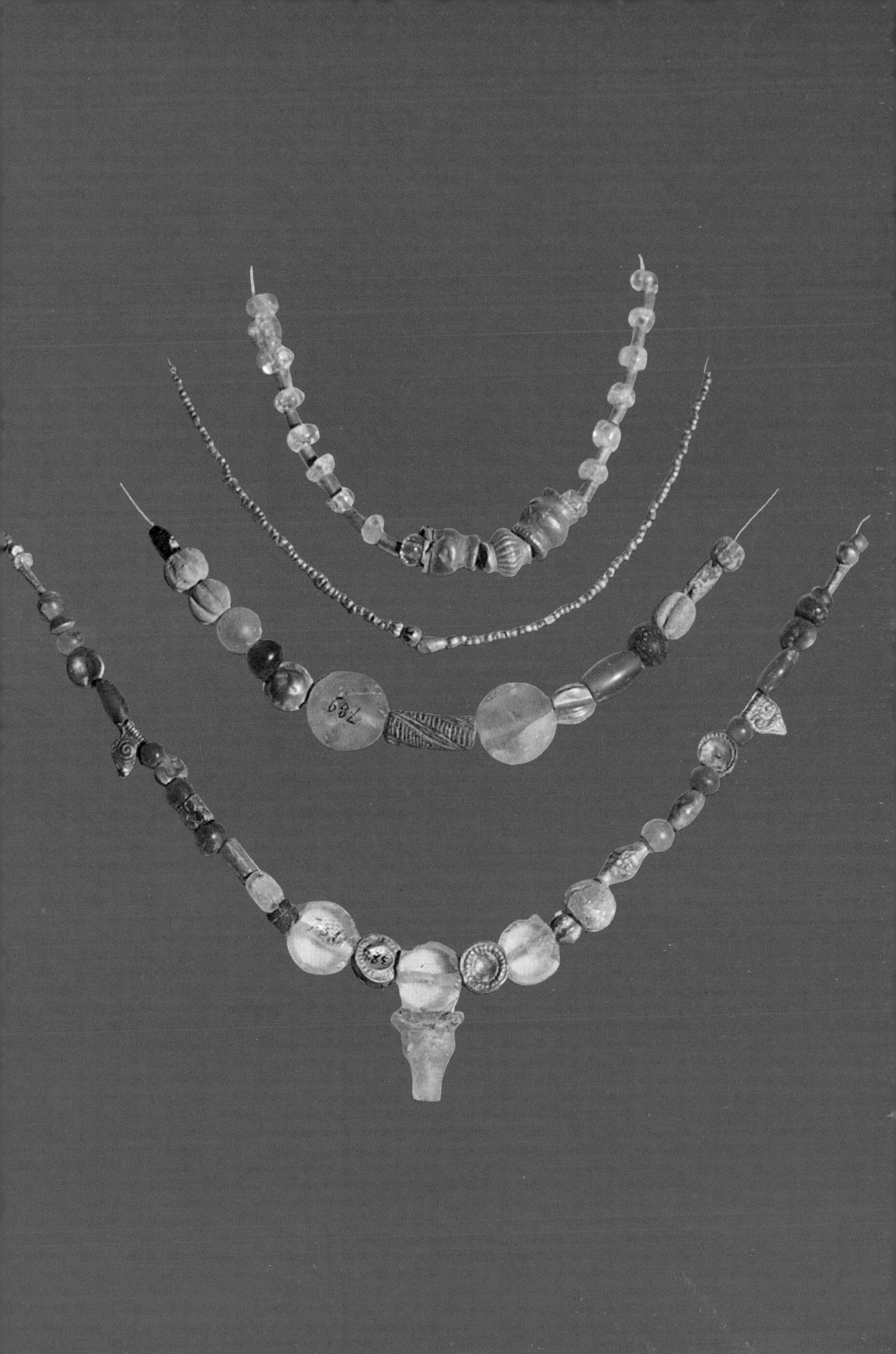

GALLERY II

Finds of the Protopalatial period (1900 - 1700 BC) from the palaces of Knossos and Malia and from peak sanctuaries in Central and Eastern Crete. Of exceptional significance are the Kamares style vases: on the shiny black surface a great variety of spiral and curvilinear motifs are painted in red and white. This style is considered to be the most beautiful in the whole of prehistoric Greece.

Case 20

On the upper shelf, curious bell-shaped objects with horn-like protrusions on the upper part, from Tylissos. It seems that they imitate masks with horns which were sometimes worn by priests in rituals.

Case 21A

Pottery, stone and bronze votives from the peak sanctuary at Youchtas, near Archanes. This shrine is connected in Greek tradition with the tomb of Zeus. Figurines, double axes, small stone altars, kernoi et al. In the next case, **21B,** a miniature gold pendant in the form of a droplet with representations of scorpion, snake and insect. It is a phylactery intended to protect its wearer from snake and insect bites.

Case 23

Fine examples of polychrome Kamares style vases from the palace of Knossos. Of especial interest are the so-called «eggshell» vases, small cups with very thin walls and wonderful decoration. They are luxury vessels, exceptionally light, which must have been made in the palace workships.

Case 24

On the upper shelf, sacred clay objects from the palace of Knossos: three small columns surmounted by doves (model of a «tricolumnar shrine» with doves, symbolising the «epiphany» of the deity), model of a litter in which the priest or idol of the goddess were borne in religious processions et al.

On the other shelves, clay figurines of worshippers which were brought by the faithful to the goddess worshipped at the peak sanctuaries. They are somewhat inartistic figurines yet nonetheless furnish us with invaluable information about the dress of the period. The men wear loincloths and sometimes have a small knife tucked in at the waist. The women wear a wide bell-shaped skirt, high-collared bodice and have elaborate coiffures. Among the other votives are members of the human body (legs, hands, breasts) which must have been offered to the goddess by sick suppliants in search of a cure. Similar «tamata» (votives of silver) are offered in Greek churches today.

Case 25

The «Town Mosaic». Small faience plaques comprising the covering of a wooden box. They depict, in considerable detail, the facades of two - and three-storeyed houses with ashlar masonry and wooden reinforcements, windows and attics or lightwells on the flat roofs.

Case 29

Large Kamares style vases from the palace of Knossos. Outstanding is the pithos with large white palms.

Kamares style pithos decorated with fishes. From the palace of Phaistos.

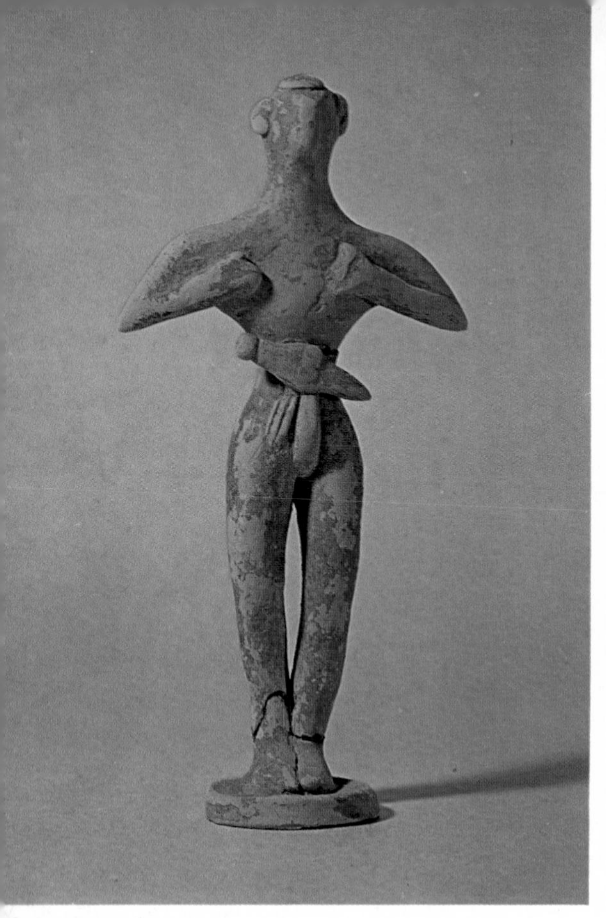

Clay male figurine from a peak sanctuary.

Clay female figurine from a peak sanctuary.

Faience plaques depicting the facades of houses. From the palace of Knossos. →

Lovely clay Kamares style vase. From the palace of Phaistos.

GALLERY III

Finds from the important **Protopalatial** phase of the palace of Phaistos. The series of Kamares style vases is exceptional.

Case 33A

Impressive cylindrical clay vessel (perhaps the base of a vase) from Paistos. On its surface there is a modelled representation of the seabed with dolphins, shells etc.

Case 34

Fine example of Kamares pottery. The diverse polychrome curvilinear motifs create an illusion of movement and rotation. Worthy of attention is the ewer with double white spiral and red spring-like motifs and the cup with «swastika», which is an astral symbol.

Case 36

Kamares vases from the palace of Phaistos. Some vases have curious and charming forms like the bowl with incorporated "cheese grater" and the «teapot» with strainer.

Case 41

The Phaistos Disk. Clay disk found in the NE sector of the palace of Phaistos and dated to the beginning of the Neopalatial period. On both faces are stamped signs of hieroglyphic script, the first form of writing used by the Minoans. The inscription has been stamped in spiral arrangement from the periphery towards the centre. Each sign registers a syllable and the words are separated from one another by vertical lines. The signs depict human figures, animals and various tools. The text has not been deciphered, even though there have been many attempts. Perhaps it is a religious hymn.

Case 42

Ritual vessels from the palace of Phaistos. On the upper shelf, a conch shell (triton) which was used as a rhyton and also as a megaphone. Below, clay tables on which liquids or fruits were placed as an offering to the deity. In the hollow of the high-footed table there is a representation of the goddess with raised arms and priestesses dancing to right and left of her.

Case 43

Large, luxurious Kamares vessels, some of the finest examples of this ware: fruit bowl with dentelated rim, impressive crater (0.50 cm. high) ornamented with relief flowers around the rim and foot, and ewer with painted decoration similar to that of the krater. Surely these must have been items which graced the royal table. On the right, a pithos with fishes and nets, a unique motif for Kamares pottery, presaging the Marine style which was to follow.

The «Phaistos Disk». Clay disk with hieroglyphic signs. From the palace of Phaistos.

Lovely clay Kamares style vase. From the palace of Phaistos.

Clay Kamares style krater with relief flowers. From the palace of Phaistos.

GALLERY IV

Finds of the Neopalatial period (1700 - 1450 BC), the most important period of the Minoan civilisation. These objects, which include several masterpieces, come from the palace of Knossos (the majority), Phaistos and Malia.

Case 46

Strange clay vessels connected with the cult of the sacred snake. According to one point of view, the sacred snakes lived in the large tubular vases and their diet of milk and honey was placed in the cups attached to their sides. However, perhaps the vases were «kernoi», i.e. vessels for offerings. On the left, model of a honeycomb with snake on top and small perforated vases with bas-relief snake motifs.

Case 47

On the second shelf, on the left, stone head of a royal mace from the palace of Malia. One edge terminates in an axe blade and the other in the bust of a leopard, the skin spots of which have been rendered with incisions.

Case 49

Pottery from the palace of Phaistos. On the upper shelf, clay rhyton in the form of a bull's head and the loveliest example of the Floral style, a ewer completely covered with dense reeds or grass. On the second shelf, elegant Marine style rhyton with nautili, seaweed and coral.

Case 50

Finds from the Temple Repositories of the palace of Knossos. On the upper shelf, small faience vessels. In the middle, the famous «Snake Goddesses», faience figurines depicting two goddesses, perhaps mother and daughter. They wear typical elegant Cretan costume consisting of long full skirt with apron and narrow bodice which leaves the breasts uncovered. The larger one has snakes around her body and arms and entwined about the tall tiara she wears on her head. The smaller one has snakes in her extended arms. A panther sits on her headdress. The small coloured shells next to them, as well as the faience models of flowers, rocks, nautili and flying fish, on the bottom shelf, would have decorated a pedestal on which the figurines would have stood.

Case 51

The most renowned Minoan work of art is the steatite libation rhyton in the form of the head of a bull, the holy animal of Minoan religion. The head has great realism and vitality. Details have been rendered in relief or incised, the eye is of rock crystal and red jasper and the nose out of nacre. The right side is authentic, while the left one is entirely restored. It was found in the Little Palace at Knossos.

Case 52

On one of the long sides, a large sword with crystal hilt from the palace of Malia. This and the mace in case 47 were used by the king when presiding over official ceremonies. On the left, gold covering of the hilt of another sword from the palace of Malia. Impressed decoration showing an acrobat whose body is so arched that the feet touch the head. On the other narrow side, on the left, rock crystal plaque with coloured representation of an acrobat leaping upon a bull.

Case 55

A few more objects from the Temple Repositories of the palace of Knossos. In the middle, a large stone «Greek» cross, sun or solar symbol. To right and left, faience plaques with scenes of a cow and wild goat suckling their young. Perhaps the Mother Goddess and her daughter appeared in the guise of a cow or goat. Another two faience objects are the models of elaborate dresses. In Minoan religion there were rites when actual dresses were presented to the goddess.

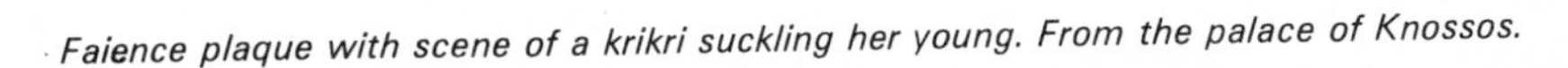

Faience plaque with scene of a krikri suckling her young. From the palace of Knossos.

Case 56

The ivory bull-leaper from the palace of Knossos, one of the masterpieces of Minoan art. It represents an agile young acrobat at the moment of performing the dangerous jump from the back of the bull. A large part of the original surface has been abraded. The holes in the head were for the attachment of gilded bronze ringlets.

Case 57

Royal gaming board resembling chess or backgammon. It is made of ivory and decorated with rock crystal, faience and glass paste (much restored). Next to it are the ivory pawns.

Case 59

Wonderful alabaster libation rhyton in the form of a lioness' head. It was found in the palace of Knossos.The eyes and nose, which are missing, were made of different material.

The «Bull-leaper». Ivory figurine of an athlete leaping over the back of a bull. From the palace of Knossos.

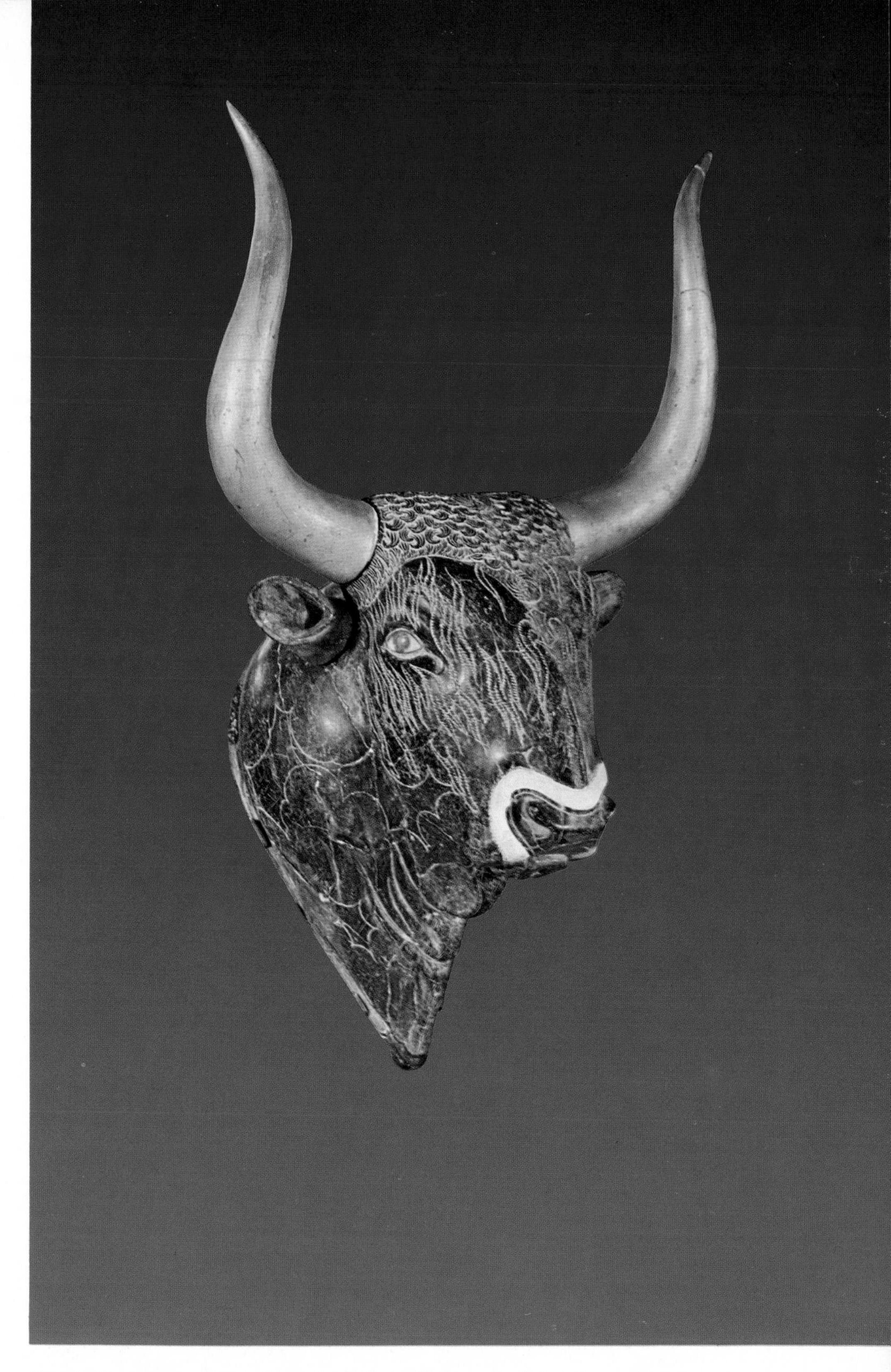

Steatite libation vessel in the form of a bull's head. From the Little Palace at Knossos.

GALLERY V

Finds from the final phase of the palace of Knossos, the era of the installation of the Mycenaean dynasty (1450 – 1380 BC).

Case 62

On the upper shelf, the stone coiffure, possibly of a wooden female statue. On the middle shelf, interesting Egyptian objects which have aided the absolute dating of the Minoan civilisation: circular alabaster pyxis lid with the name of the Hyksos pharaoh Kyan in hieroglyphics, statuette of a seated male figure, the Egyptian official User and stone vases. On the bottom shelf; a large piece of porphyry in the form of a pyramid with bas - relief decoration of an octopus. Perhaps it was a «standard» weight i.e. it was used to control the weight of bronze «talants» which were the units of exchange at that time. Recently, this piece, which has a hole at the top, has been interpreted as an anchor. Next to it, is the lower part of a small votive column with bas-relief ivy-leaf decoration. On the right, two tall porphyry oil lamps. The hollow in the centre was for the oil and the two spouts at the edges for the wicks.

Case 66

Below, alabaster vessels (squat «alabastra») from the Throne Room of the palace of Knossos. Apparently these were being used in a rite performed shortly before the final catastrophic blow to the palace in 1380 BC.

Case 69

On one side, tablets and other objects from different regions. All bear Linear A inscriptions, the script which replaced hieroglyphic writing and was in use during the Neopalatial period. This script has not yet been deciphered and so we can only guess at the contents of the tablets.

On the other side of the case, tablets from the palace of Knossos with Linear B inscriptions. This script, which is a modification of Linear A, was employed at Knossos during the period of Mycenaean domination as well as in the Mycenaean palaces of the Greek Mainland. Its decipherment in 1952 by the English scholars M. Ventris and J. Chadwick demonstrated that it renders the oldest form of the Greek language, the Mycenaean dialect. Written down on these tablets is part of the palace property: flocks of animals, agricultural produce, weapons et al. Mention is made also of men and women, surely slaves.

Case 70A

Clay house model from Archanes which furnishes much interesting information about Minoan domestic architecture. Represented, is a single-storey house with small rooms, lightwell, small windows and ramp leading to the roof terrace which was covered by a light roof, perhaps of reeds. On one side of the terrace there is a stepped verandah.

← *The famous Snake Goddesses. Faience figurines from the temple repositories of the palace of Knossos.*

Clay Linear B tablet.

Porphyry oil lamp.

Clay Linear A tablet.

GALLERY VI

Finds from tombs of the final Neopalatial and Postpalatial period (1450 - 1300 BC) in the areas of Knossos, Archanes and Phaistos.

Case 71

Three interesting clay models connected with the cult of the dead from the tholos tomb at Kamilaris, near Phaistos. One depicts a dinner offered to the dead, the other, men dancing within a circular building with horns of consecration and the third, offerings from worshippers to the deified dead who are seated and have offering tables in front of them.

Case 75A

Skeleton of a horse, just as it was found in the royal tholos tomb at Archanes. The horse had been sacrificed, dismembered and left in front of the burial chamber as an offering to the dead.

Case 78

Helmet from the Postpalatial tomb at Zapher Papoura, Knossos. It consists of boar's tusks which were sewn onto a leather cap. Such helmets were usually worn by Mycenaean warriors and it is natural that they should be found in Crete during the era of its Mycenaean domination.

Case 79A

Ivory pyxis found in the tomb at Katsamba, the ancient harbour of Knossos. A veritable masterpiece is the relief representation of the capture of a wild bull by armed hunters.

Case 80

Elegant ewer with impressive modelled decoration of spiked protruberances (perhaps imitating nails) and small figure-of-eight shields on the neck. The decoration is completed with painted schematic nautili and papyrus blossoms. This was surely a ritual vessel.

Case 82

On the bottom shelf, lovely Egyptian alabaster amphora with cartouche of the great pharaoh Tuthmoses III: it must have contained aromatic oils and would have been sent to the king of Knossos as a gift. Double pottery incense burners with charcoal, just as they were found inside the tombs. They were used periodically to purify and perfume the tombs.

Case 84

Different weapons (sword, daggers, knives, arrows) from the tombs at Zapher Papoura and the Sanatorio, Knossos. These weapons, resembling others found in Mycenaean Greece, are yet further evidence of the presence of the war-loving Mycenaeans in Crete. The abundance of weapons in tombs of this period is characteristic, in marked contrast to their virtual absence from tombs of the preceding periods, when the «Pax Minoica» prevailed throughout the island.

Case 87

Gold jewellery from various cemeteries: gold mask for covering the face of the dead, with very fine granular decoration, and the famous gold seal ring from the great royal tomb at Isopata, Knossos. Engraved on the bezel is a representation of a goddess descending from heaven, while priestesses enact a ritual dance in a meadow of lilies.

Case 88

Finds from tombs in the highly significant cemetery at Phourni, Archanes: Luxurious necklaces with beads of gold, glass paste and sard in a diversity of shapes. A fine gold sealring with scene of a sacred tree worship. Bronze mirror with ivory handle and small gold boxes, perhaps phylacteries. Also, pieces of ivory from the inlaid decoration of a wooden footstool: large and small figure-of-eight shields, plaques with busts of warriors with helmets et al.

Ivory pyxis with relief representation of the capture of a bull. From Katsamba.

Clay libation jug from Katsamba.

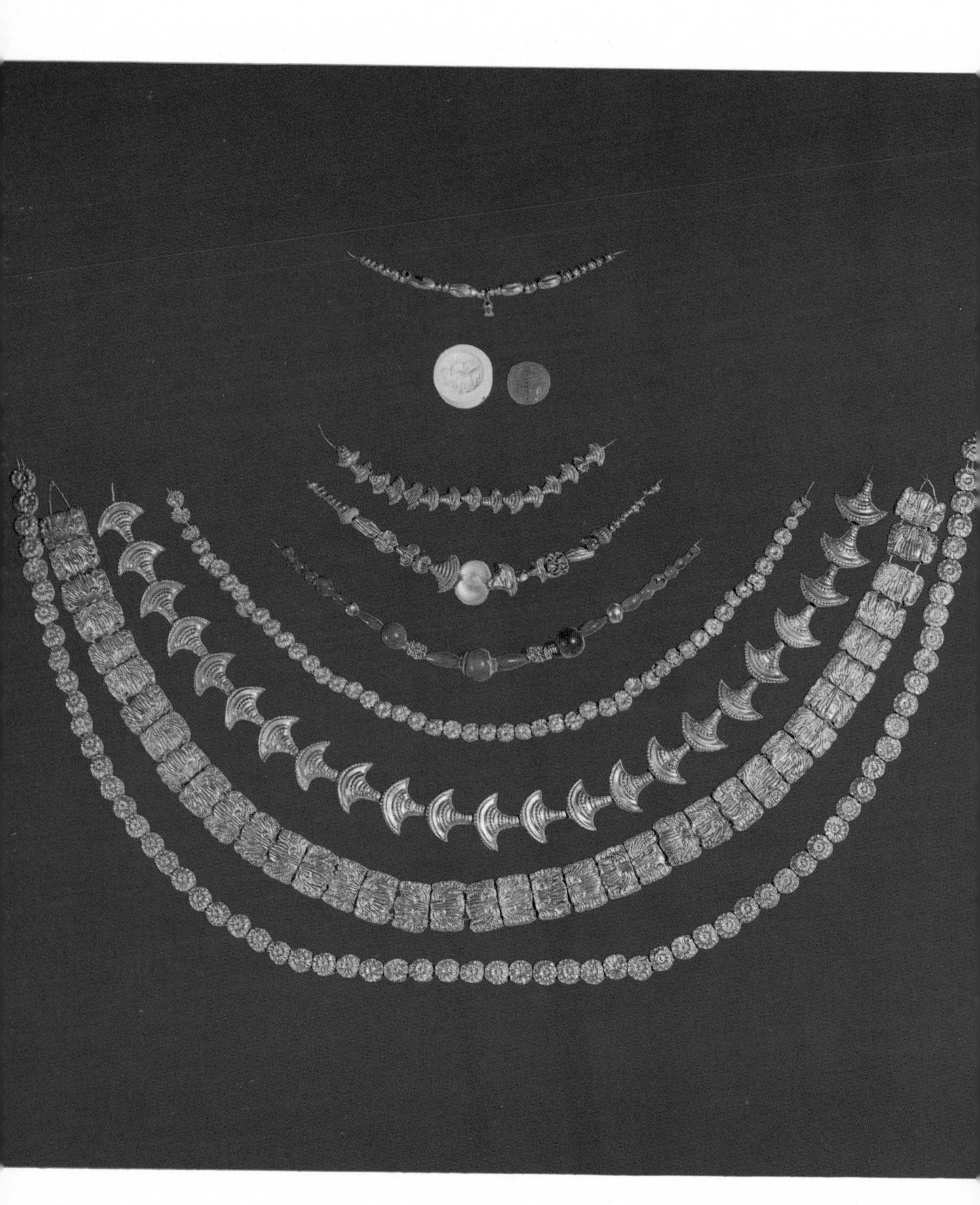

Necklaces of gold and semiprecious stones, from Archanes.

GALLERY VII

Finds, principally of the Neopalatial period, from megara, villas and sacred caves of Central Crete. Some of them rank among the most significant Minoan works of art.

To the right of the entrance three enormous bronze double axes from the megaron at Nirou are displayed. They have been set on modern bases and pedestals which, however, are copies of the axe bases illustrated on the famous Aghia Triada sarcophagus. The double axe was the most important symbol in Minoan religion. It is frequently shown in representations accompanying the Great Goddess or between sacral horns or bull' s horns. There are also many examples of actual double axes, usually votives and, more rarely, for use in cult.

Case 94

The famous «Harvesters' Vase» from the villa of Aghia Triada. It is made of steatite in the form of an ostrich egg (the lower portion is restored). It is decorated with a bas-relief scene of a procession of men with their harvesting implements on their shoulders. The procession, which was probably an act of thanksgiving to the deity for the rich harvest, is accompanied by four musicians who sing while their leader plucks the sistrum with small bells and beats out the rhythm.

Case 95

Steatite vase known as the «Chieftain's Cup» or «Cup of the Report», from the royal villa at Aghia Triada. Depicted is a young king or prince, mace in hand, listening to a report delivered by the officer standing directly in front of him. This officer is perhaps offering the king the animal hides which the three men on the back face of the vase are holding.

Case 96

Conical steatite rhyton, also from the villa at Aghia Triada. The surface is divided into four zones with relief representations of athletic contests which were perhaps held on the occasion of a major religious festival. In the first, third and fourth zone wrestling and boxing contests are shown with great vitality. In the second zone there is a scene of bull-leaping where the acrobats jump over the back of a charging bull.

Case 97

Enormous bronze swords and double axes, offerings to the goddess (perhaps of a martial nature) who was worshipped in the sacred cave of Arkalochori.

Case 98

A few more large votive axes from the Arkalochori cave. One of the axes bears a hieroglyphic inscription with signs similar to those on the Phaistos disk.

Case 99

Copper «talants» from the villa at Aghia Triada. Each one weighs 29.5 kilos and it seems that they were used as units of exchange. Their shape, with concave sides, was probably to facilitate carrying them on the shoulder. Some of them have signs in the Minoan or Cypriot script incised on them. It is very probable that they were all imported from Cyprus, major centre of copper production in prehistoric times.

Case 101

Gold jewellery from different places. The most important and best - known item is the bee pendant from the cemetery of Chrysolakkos, near Malia. Two bees or wasps deposit a droplet of honey in the honeycomb which is rendered as a disc with granular decoration. In addition to granulation, repoussé and filigrane techniques were used. Equally charming are the periapts in the form of a seated lion, a duck and a fish. Of especial interest is a phylactery from Aghia Triada with representation of a human hand, snake, spider and scorpion. Similar is the phylactery from Youchta in case 21B. The small gold double axes on the north side of the case are votives from the Arkalochori cave.

The famous gold ornament in the form of two bees. From the cemetery of Chrysolakkos at Malia.

← *The «Harvesters' Vase». Steatite vase with relief representation of an agricultural religious procession. From the Villa at Aghia Triada.*

GALLERY VIII

Finds from the excavations at the palace of Zakros in Eastern Crete (1600 - 1450 BC). Worthy of special attention are the stone ritual vessels. On the west wall there is a plaster frieze of relief spirals which embellished the palace Hall of religious Banquets.

Case 109

Wonderful rock crystal rhyton. At the base of the neck there is a ring of crystal and pieces of ivory covered with gold leaf. The handle consists of crystal beads which nowadays have a greenish colour due to the oxidation of the bronze wire connecting them. It was found in the Temple Repository.

Case 111

Greenstone rhyton with impressive relief decoration of a peak sanctuary. On the main face, the portal of the shrine, decorated with spirals, two pairs of krikri on top of the roof, birds flying or perched upon the horns of consecration, altars, precinct et al. are shown. On the back face there is a rocky landscape, wherein the shrine is located, and goats scampering in different directions.

Case 112

Large bronze cult axe with double blades on each side. Its surface is ornamented with incised stylised lilies.

Case 113

On the upper shelf, two «Floral style» cups and an elegant «Marine style» ewer with numerous small nautili. On the lower shelf, two elephant tusks which must have been imported as raw material from Syria. Copper «talants» (ingots), perhaps from Cyprus.

Case 114

Wonderful series of stone conical rhytons from the Temple Repositories.

Case 116

Greenstone libation vessel in the form of a bull's head. The eyes, which would have been of a different material, are missing. The horns are plaster-of-Paris copies of the original gilded wooden ones. It is reminiscent of the famous bull's head rhyton from Knossos.

Case 118

Some ritual vessels from the Temple Repositories: «Communion chalices» (one is of obsidian), rhytons, an impressive limestone amphora with high elegant handles. Also rhytons of faience in the form of a bull's head and stone hammers which were held by the priests during rites.

Wonderful rock crystal rhyton. From the palace of Zakros.

Stone rhyton with relief representation of a peak sanctuary. From the palace of Zakros.

Polychrome stone amphora with high handles and double mouth. From the palace of Zakros. →

GALLERY IX

Finds of the Neopalatial period (1700 - 1450 BC) from Eastern Crete. They come from the settlements at Palaikastro, Gournia, Pseira and the peak sanctuary at Piskokephalo.

Case 120

Perhaps the loveliest example of Marine style pottery is the flask decorated with an octopus, the tentacles of which embrace the entire vase. Below, «kernos» for offerings of liquids or fruits to the goddess.

Case 123

Clay male and female figurines from the peak sanctuary at Piskokephalo, Siteia. They are shown in attitudes of worship, usually with hands on the breast, and are amongst the loveliest examples of Minoan clay sculpture. The elaborate female coiffures are particularly impressive. Below, clay models of the beetle «Rhinoceros oryctes», which the Minoans regarded as sacred.

Case 128

Seals of the Neopalatial period made of various semi-precious stones (amethyst, sard, agate, rock crystal, haematite et al). They are among the finest examples of Minoan carved gems. With unique artistry diverse subjects such as animals, solitary or in compositions, sacred symbols and vessels and many interesting religious scenes with priests or priestesses et al; have been carved on the seal face.

Clay female statuette, votive at a peak sanctuary.

Flask decorated with an octapus. From ***Palaikastro.***

GALLERY X

Finds representative of the Postpalatial civilisation (1380 - 1100 BC). The absence of luxury materials and stylisation are the characteristics of these works of art.

Case 132

Clay model of a sacred dance. Women hold each other by the shoulder and dance, while a female musician plays the lyre. The representation brings to mind present-day Cretan dances. On the same shelf, a censer and perforated cover of an incense burner with decoration of birds.

Case 133

Characteristic female idols of the Postpalatial era, from the sanctuary at Gazi, Herakleion. They are large cult idols, the lower part of the body is cylindrical and the arms raised in an attitude of supplication, blessing or «epiphany» («goddess with raised arms»). The head is adorned with different symbols such as birds and horns of consecration. The largest goddess has opium poppy pods on her head, the juice of which seeds would have induced a state of ecstasy in the worshippers.

Case 139

Steatite and schist moulds for making jewellery and holy objects of metal or glass paste. The moulds from Siteia were used for the manufacture of figurines of deities and various religious symbols.

Case 142

Idols of the goddess with raised arms, from Gournia and Prinia. Tubular vessels with snake-like handles and relief representations of sacral horns. They are considered as having been the dwellings of sacred snakes, libation vessels or as bases on which cups of offerings were placed.

The «Poppy Goddess». Clay figurine of a female deity from the shrine of Gazi with poppies on her head.

GALLERY XI

Finds of the Subminoan and Protogeometric period (1100 - 900 BC) which were eras of artistic impoverishment and decline.

Case 145

Typical vases of the Protogeometric period, decorated with simple geometric motifs. Of interest is the annular Kernos with miniature amphorae and between them human figures.

Case 148

Large clay idols of the goddess with raised arms which were found in the Subminoan settlement at Karphi, Lasithi. They represent the final phase in the development of this type and have a distorted face and exaggeration of certain parts of the body. The cylindrical dress has square holes through which separately modelled clay feet protruded. Also curious is the libation vase in the form of a cart drawn by oxen, only the heads of which have been rendered.

Case 149

Various votives from the cave of Eileithyia, goddess of fecundity and parturition, at Inatos. The majority are of the Geometric period though some Minoan religious symbols, such as the double axe, are used indicating that the old Minoan tradition has not completely disappeared. Most of the figurines are connected with the theme of reproduction: erotic couples, pregnant women and others with babe in arms.

Case 153

Iron weapons and tools from Geometric tombs. As is well-known, during this period iron appeared for the first time and replaced bronze. On the other side of the case, a display of fibulae, used as a shoulder fastening and ornament for the Doric peplos, which had replaced the Minoan costume with flounced skirt and narrow bodice.

Case 157

Large vases of an advanced phase of the Geometric period with more complex geometric motifs (spirals, rosettes, meanders etc.)· One is a funerary urn (since cremation of the dead was by that time widespread) and the other two are amphorae.

Clay rhyton in the form of a cart drawn by oxen. From Karfi, Lasithi. →

GALLERY XII

Finds of the mature Geometric period and «Orientalising» period (900 - 650 BC); Of especial interest is the pottery, particularly of the Orientalising period, and the metalwork.

Case 161A

Votives from the recent excavations in the sanctuary of Hermes and Aphrodite at Kato Symi, Viannos. Other votives from the sanctuary, which began life in Minoan times and continued through until the Hellenistic era, are exhibited in cases 160, 161 and 161B. In this case there is a most important series of sheet-bronze cut-out figures, mainly of Archaic times, interesting examples of the advanced metalwork of the period. The cut-outs were affixed to small wooden plaques which were hung in the sanctuary (something like the plaquettes with the reconstructions which hang on the walls above the case). They represent male figures, some with himation and short sceptre, others with loincloth or himation on the shoulder and bow and quiver. They are all worshippers bringing animals as offerings to the god.

Case 163

Pottery of the «Orientalising» period from the ancient city of Arkades (present-day Aphrati). The influence of Anatolian art is particularly pronounced during this period. Complex floral motifs, lions, imaginary animals such as sphinxes, griffins et al; enrich the old, somewhat austere, Geometric repertoire. Scenes with human figures are also depicted quite frequently. Outstanding is the funerary urn with representation of the deceased and his wife in an attitutude of lament, and the oinochoe on which a loving couple, perhaps the mythical lovers Theseus and Ariadne, is depicted.

Case 167

Geometric funerary urns, typical finds from the cemetery at Fortetsa, near Knossos. The usual geometric motifs are meanders, zig-zag lines, concentric circles, braids, birds etc. The polychrome decoration on Geometric vases is characteristic of the Knossos region. Designs were painted in blue and red on the white slip of the surface.

Case 168

Orientalising pottery from the cemetery of Arkades (see case 163). Worthy of special attention are three vases with interesting representations: cylindrical urn with a male figure leading a horse, another urn with winged figure between sphinxes (perhaps the mythical giant Talos who guarded the shores of Crete) and a bell-shaped funerary urn with the Mother goddess between wading birds.

Case 170

Gold jewellery from the Geometric tomb of Tekes, Knossos. It has neither the finesse nor charm of Minoan jewellery but these are, nonetheless, interesting examples of Geometric goldsmithing and indicate an advanced technique. Crescent-shaped rock crystal pendant with chain from which the lunar symbol and solar disc hang. Pendant of a cross within a crescent with human heads as finials. Necklace of large rock crystal beads. Gold band with repeated repoussé design of a god taming a lion.

Clay oinochoe with representation of a loving couple, perhaps Theseus and Ariadne.

← *Pieces of jewellery of the Geometric period, of gold and rock crystal.*

GALLERY XIII

In the SE corner of the gallery there is an extraordinary wooden maquette of the palace of Knossos. It gives a wonderful picture of the multi-storeyed new palace with hundreds of rooms, staircases, magnificent entrances, large courts etc.

On display in the rest of the gallery are clay sarcophagi from different cemeteries. The majority are of the Postpalatial period when the custom of burying the dead in clay coffins, instead of wooden ones which were in use during the two preceding periods, was widespread in Crete. There are two types of sacrophagi: the box-shaped with lid and the bathtub shaped. They are usually small because the dead were interred therein in a contracted position. Subjects chosen for the painted decoration of the sarcophagi were similar to those used in contemporary vase painting: stylised flowers, birds, fish et al. Of especial interest are some sarcophagi decorated with cult scenes.

Clay box-shaped sarcophagus from Vasilika Anogeia.

GALLERY XIV

In this and the next two galleries there is an exhibition of the wall-paintings which embellished the walls of the palace of Knossos and other wealthy houses or villas of the Neopalatial period. Only small pieces have survived, which have been completed and the whole composition restored with relative accuracy. The pictures were painted on fresh plaster (fresco) with mineral pigments (black, white, red, yellow and blue). A variation of the wall-painting is the coloured relief. The subjects are usually scenes from nature or religious rituals. The male figures are painted red and the women white. Freedom, charm, imagination and love of colour are the characteristic features of Minoan wall-paintings.

To the left, on the north side of the gallery, sections of the wall-painting which adorned the long Corridor of the Procession in the palace of Knossos. Young men clad in luxurious loincloths, holding vases in their hands, advance in single file from two directions towards the centre, where the princess or priestess representing the great goddess, is portrayed («Procession of Giftbearers»). The figure at the very end, of which the head is preserved, is known as the **Rhyton bearer.**

Next, between the two doors, is the fire-blackened and much destroyed fragments of the wall-painting which decorated the Throne Room in the palace of Knossos. A large winged **griffin** with eagle's head, lion's body and snake's tail is depicted between papyrus flowers.

The wall-paintings which follow, on the same wall, come from the opulent villa of Aghia Triada, near Phaistos. The loveliest is that showing a **wild cat** amidst lush vegetation preparing to pounce on a pheasant which sits, unsuspectingly, on a rock. The final fresco of the series depicts a **marine environment** with dolphins and octopus and decorated the floor of a shrine.

On the opposite wall, starting from the west, the following wall-paintings are displayed: **White lilies and red irises** from Amnissos. The well-known **«Bull sports fresco»** from Knossos with male and female athletes at various stages in the games. The **frieze with partridges** from the Caravanserai at Knossos. Bands with composition of spirals. The **blue dolphins** from the Queen's megaron in the palace of Knossos. The **Blue ladies** with luxurious garments and jewellery. The wonderful relief **Bull's head** from the north entrance to the palace of Knossos. The famous **«Prince with the Lilies»,** a young king or prince-priest with magnificent crown of lily flowers and peacock plumes. Large **figure-of-eight shields.**

In the middle of the gallery stands the famous stone **sarcophagus from Aghia Triada,** one of the most important exhibits in the museum. On all four plastered sides there is painted decoration of scenes connected with the cult of the deified of heroised royal dead. On one long side, a scene showing the sacrifice of a bull. The victim is tied to a table, beneath which there are two other animals also destined for sacrifice. The sacrifice is witnessed by priestesses and a musician with double flute. There is a priestess clad in skins offering a libation from a ewer and fruits from a basket, in front of the precinct of a sacred tree.

«Blue Ladies». Wall-painting from the palace of Knossos.

Wall-painting with scene of bull-leaping, from the palace of Knossos.

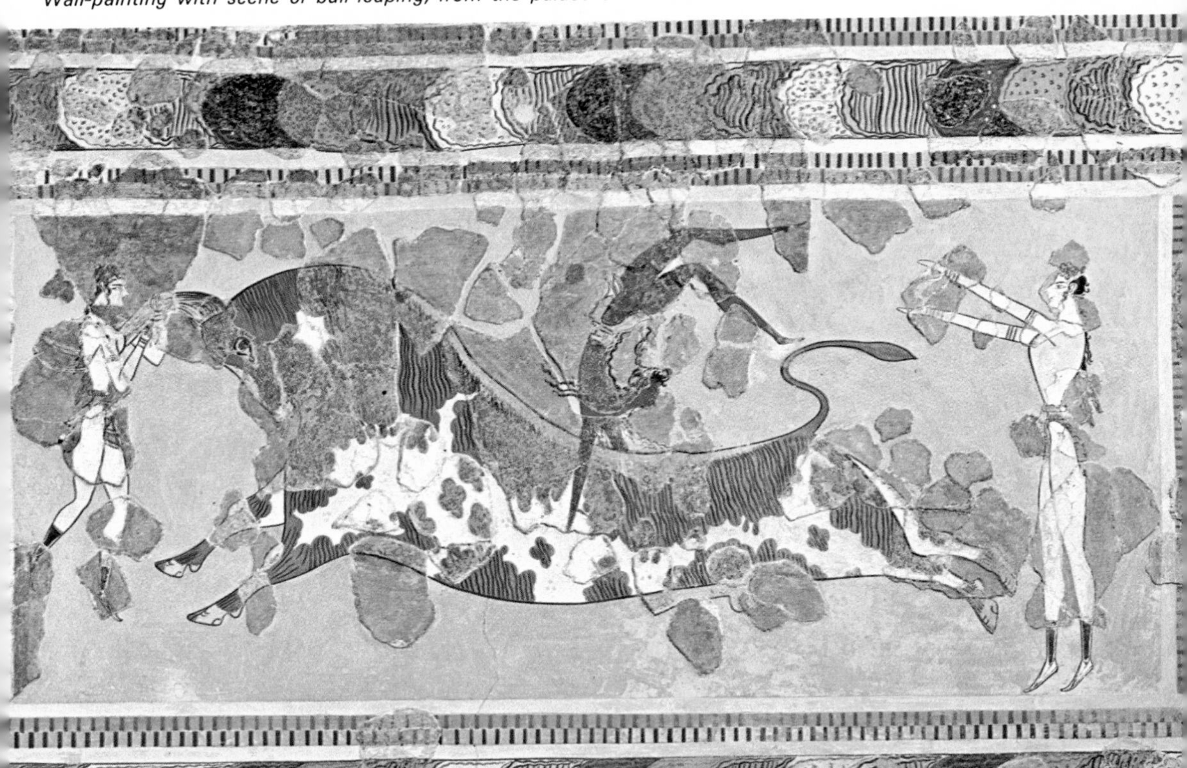

On the other long side, a musician with lyre and a priestess with crown and wooden yoke over her shoulder from which buckets are suspended. There is a second priestess who is perhaps pouring the blood of the sacrificed animal into a large receptacle between tall double axes. In the other half of this side priests wearing animal skins are shown holding calves and a boat in their arms and offering these to the dead, who is illustrated completely covered in animal skins in front of his tomb. There is a sacred tree and an altar in the foreground.

On both the narrow sides a chariot with two figures is depicted. One is drawn by winged griffins and the other by horses.

The sarcophagus is dated to the first half of the 14th century BC.

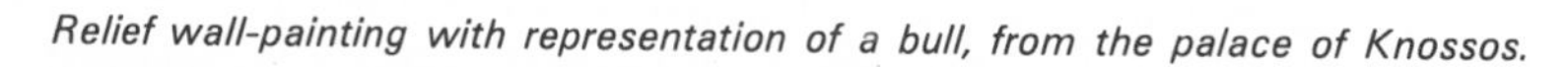

Relief wall-painting with representation of a bull, from the palace of Knossos.

*'he «Rhyton Bearer». Figure from
'he wall-painting of the
'ift-bearers from the palace of
'nossos.*

«Frieze with partridges». Wall-painting from the Caravanserai of Knossos.

Stone sarcophagus from Aghia Triada with painted scenes of the cult of the dead.

GALLERY XV

The most significant frescoes are those from Knossos, which are exhibited on the west wall. The first two are **miniature wall-paintings,** i.e. the human figures are illustrated on a small scale. One depicts priestesses in a ritual dance in a sacred grove, while the crowd observes, and the other a festival in the «Tripartite shrine» of the palace. There follows the well-known **«Parisienne»,** as the workers named the charming young priestess with the sacral knot in the nape of her neck. It belongs, together with other fragments which have survived and are exhibited next to it, to a composition representing offerings of holy kylixes to seated priestly figures.

GALLERY XVI

On the east wall there are wall-paintings from the **«House of the Frescoes»** at Knossos. The **Blue Bird** and **Blue Monkeys** amidst veined rocks and lush vegetation.

On the west wall, outstanding are: the **Dancing Girl** with her hair billowing freely as she twirls around, and the **Saffron Gatherer,** blue monkey picking crocuses. As we can see in the reconstruction beside it, the pithecoid figure was originally thought to be human (the «Blue Boy»).

GALLERY XVII

Yamalakis Collection.

Objects in the Collection of the Herakliote physician S. Yamalakis which was purchased by the Greek State in 1962. It includes pottery, stone vases, figurines, bronze weapons and tools, jewellery, seal stones and other objects of all periods.

Outstanding: Neolithic clay figurine of a seated female figure, from Hierapetra (case 175). Bronze figurine of a young male with a calf on his shoulders (case 178). Clay model of a Protogeometric shrine in which there sits a goddess with raised arms, while two males look down from the roof (case 181). Minoan seals of semiprecious stones and Babylonian cylinder seals (cases 187 and 188).

Three gold artefacts from the Zakros region: bull's head with rosette between the horns, diadem with representation of a goddess taming krikris and a shallow dish.

Clay Neolithic figurine of a seated female figure, from Hierapetra.

← *«La Parisienne». Wall-painting from the palace of Knossos with representation of a young priestess.*

GALLERY XVIII

Small artefacts of the Archaic, Classical, Hellenistic and Greco-Roman period (7th century BC - 4th century AD). Terracotta and bronze figurines, bronze weapons, vases, jewellery, coins et al.

Case 193

Terracotta figurines of the goddess Athena from the Archaic shrine deposit at Gortyn. The goddess wears a tall helmet and holds a spear and shield.

Case 194

Ritual vessels from the Archaic shrine deposit at Gortyn. They include kernoi, vessels with several hollows within which small quantities of agricultural produce were placed as a thanksgiving to the deity. They are associated with the cult of Demeter. Similar kernoi were used during Minoan times.

Case 197

Bronze cuirass from Arkades (present-day Aphrati). The small size indicates that it belonged to a child.

Case 198

Assorted bronze vessels from Fortetsa, Knossos and the Idaean cave. Of especial interest is the Archaic helmet from Axos. It is embellished with a wonderful relief representation of winged horses and rosettes.

Case 200

Vessels from the deposit of the shrine of Demeter at Gortyn. The large oil lamps with multiple spouts for wicks were used in special rituals. The terracotta figurines are of men with piglets (sacred animal of Demeter) in their arms and women with baskets of holy vessels on the head.

Case 201

Terracotta winged Cupids and models of ostrich eggs from the Hellenistic tomb of a maiden at Gortyn.

In the NW corner of the gallery stands the magnificent bronze statue of a youth, from Hierapetra. It is dated to the 1st century BC.

Case 203

A special accessory of the Cretan suit of armour was the «mitra», the semicircular girdle which protected the abdomen. The mitrae usually bore engraved or impressed decoration, as on those from Axos which are exhibited in this case. They are ornamented with scenes of athletes, animals, tripod cauldrons et al.

Clay figurine of Athena with helmet, from Gortyn. →

GALLERY XIX

Monumental art of the Archaic period (7th - 6th century BC).

Archaic Cretan sculpture occupies a special place in the history of early Greek sculpture. Indeed, Crete has been considered by many scholars as the birthplace of the large sculptures known as «Daedalic». In this gallery there are many notable works, including some which are unique.

High up on the west wall is a large stone frieze from the temple on the acropolis of Prinias. It depicts horsemen with shields and javelins (3rd quarter of 6th century BC). Beneath the frieze, two large rectangular plaques from Gortyn with representation of a triad of deities. The female deities are completely nude except for a tall headdress, the «polos» (circa 650 BC).

On the north side of the gallery, the torso of Eleutherne (630 - 620 BC) and two poros-stone bird models from Amnissos (Zeus' eagle and Hera's hawk). On the north door, which leads to the adjacent room, the internal pylon or portal of the temple at Prinias has been reassembled. Above the lintel are two seated figures of a goddess, perhaps Rhea (3rd quarter of 7th century BC). Below right, funerary stelae from Prinias with incised decoration, which were incorporated within grave structures above ground level.

In about the middle of the room (case 210) three bronze statuettes from the temple of Apollo at Dreros are exhibited. The technique of hammering was used for their manufacture and they depict Apollo, his mother Leto and his sister Artemis (1st half of 7th century BC).

In cases 208 and 209 important examples of Cretan metalworking from the Idaean cave, where, according to mythology, Zeus was raised, are displayed. They include votive shields, cymbals and shallow bowls with interesting relief representations. The oriental influence is particularly marked in both technique and subjects. On one cymbal Zeus is shown in the centre stepping on a bull and dismembering a lion. To right and left Curetes demons clash their cymbals.

Bronze cymbal from the Ida cave with relief representation of Zeus and Curetes.

On the south wall, the famous hymn of Zeus Cretogenis, inscribed on the black stone stele found at Palaikastro, Siteia. The inscription was made in Roman times though the text of the hymn is much older.

GALLERY XX

Greek and Greco-Roman sculptures (5th century BC - 4th century AD).

Although in Archaic times sculpture in Crete was highly developed, in Classical times, which was an era of incessant civil strife between the cities of the island, this development was cut short and very few works of note were created. There are only three Classical works in this gallery: The 5th century BC funerary stele with the young archer, from Achlada (145), the metope from the Classical temple at Knossos with the scene of Herakles and the Erymanthian boar (363) and the large 4th century funerary stele with the scene of the wife and son of the deceased bidding him farewell.

The rest of the sculptures in the gallery belong to the period when Crete was a Roman province and prospered. Gortyn, the capital of the island during that period, is the provenance of the majority, Outstanding: the larger than life-size statue of Pythios Apollo at the far end of the gallery (326). Pluto and Persephone with Cerberus between them (259 - 260), Venus with a basin in her hands (154), a copy of the Doryphoros of Polykleitos (343), fine examples of Roman portraiture, philosopher or physician with scrolls beside his left foot (1), headless statue of Venus (349), mosaic floor representing Neptune with his trident upon a seahorse et al.

On the west side of the gallery, finds from Roman Knossos: headless statue of the Emperor Hadrian in full armour (5), small statue of Bacchus crowned with an ivy wreath and pine cones (315), marble sarcophagus with relief representations.

Funerary stele of a young archer, from Achlada.

On the east side, a large sarcophagus from Malia with lovely relief representations (387), statue of a kore from Kissamos, Chania (2), two statuettes from the composition depicting Diana shooting arrows at Niobe's children (265 - 266). et al.

Statue of Aphrodite with a basin in her arms. From Gortyn.

THE PALACE OF PHAISTOS

This is the second Minoan palace both in size (8400 sq. m.) and importance. It is located in the western part of the fertile Mesara plain, built upon a hill which had control of the entrance to the plain from the south shores of Crete.

Excavations commenced in 1900 and were conducted by the Italian Archaeological School (F. Halbherr, L. Pernier and later D. Levi). Of particular significance is the fact that a large part of the first palace has been uncovered, which has furnished invaluable information about Protopalatial architecture and a wonderful series of «Kamares» vases.

Ancient tradition connects Phaistos with Rhadhamanthys, one of the two brothers of Minos, King of Knossos. A palace was built for the first time in 1900 BC and in about 1700 BC it was destroyed by an earthquake. A new, luxurious palace was built immediately, on the same site. After its final destruction in around 1450 BC, some parts of it were reoccupied by private individuals and life in the region continued until about 150 BC when Phaistos was destroyed in an attack by neighbouring Gortyn.

The remains visible at Phaistos today mainly belong to the palace of the Neopalatial period. In the West Wing, however, parts of the first palace of the Protopalatial period can also be seen.

As in the other Minoan palaces, here too there are two principal courts: the West, from which one entered the palace and the Central, with the important quarters around it. The most significant wings are the West and North.

West Wing

One enters from the **Upper Court** (91) which perhaps functioned as an «agora» or market place. A staircase in the east sector (6) leads to the **West Court** which is nowadays on two levels. The lower, which is paved and traversed by a «processional causeway» with raised flagstones, belongs to the Protopalatial period. The higher, unpaved, is part of the court of the Neopalatial period, when the West Court was considerably enlarged and the West facade displaced eastwards. In the north sector of the court there is a flight of 8 very wide steps which terminates at a high dentelated wall, comprising the **Theatral Space** of the palace. The spectators would have watched the ceremonies performed in the West Court from the steps-tiers. The king's throne would have been placed on the spot where the processional causeway, which continues up the steps, ends.

At the SE edge of the Theatre there are traces of a **Protopalatial shrine** with one main and three secondary rooms with benches. Many ritual vessels were discovered in these rooms, such as offering tables, stone vessels and a conch (triton) shell which the priests would have used as a megaphone when addressing the crowd.

Along the length of the east side of the West Court part of the facade of the first palace, with its orthostats, is preserved. A branch of the processional causeway leads to the entrance of the first palace, a propylon with column. In this region and further south, beyond the present-day fence, several rooms of the first palace are preserved to an appreciable height.

The facade of the new palace is truly impressive. A magnificent staircase (66) 13.5 m. wide with low, broad treads, leads to the **West Propylon,** the official entrance of the palace. The propylon consists of a central column (its large stone base has survived) between jambs (67). There follows a narrow space with two lofty openings (68), another space with three columns in front (69) and a lightwell (69a). These spaces have recently been considered as having been the Throne Room, which is highly probable, if we take into consideration the monumental entrance leading to them.

We go down a small staircase to the east of the lightwell, to a lower level where there is a **corridor** with central pillar (26) and **row of magazines** (27 - 37). These magazines would have comprised part of the shrine, just like the magazines in the West Wing of the palace of Knossos. The magazine at the very end of the north row (33) has been roofed and gives us an idea of what the others were like. It contains large pithoi, a clay stool, a cist or receptacle beneath the floor to collect the oil or wine accidentally spilt, and a raised corridor. East of the magazine complex a luxurious hall (25) with floor and dado of gypsum and internal columns was perhaps for religious rituals, even though it is also referred to as the **Lobby** of the magazines. Further south, a wide paved corridor united the West with the Central Court.

In the south sector of the wing are the **Religious Quarters:** rooms in which cult vessels were found (8 - 11), lustral basins (19, 21) and three rooms with facade onto the Central Court. Two of them had benches (23, 24), while the third (22) had two pillars, which must have had cultic significance, like the pillars in the crypts of the palace of Knossos.

Central Court

Its dimensions are 51.50 × 22.30 m. and it was paved with limestone flags. On its west and east side there were porticoes, the west one was later abolished. These porticoes provided shade during the hot summer days and from them the athletic contests and religious ceremonies taking place in the court could be observed.

In the NW corner there is a stepped structure which is thought to have been an altar or platform for bull-leaping. In the second instance, the bull would have placed its forelegs on the lower step, while the athlete would have stood on the upper step ready to seize the beast by its horns and embark on his dangerous leap.

East Wing

Only a small part of the East Wing has survived because the rest has collapsed and fallen down the steep hillside. It is a charming little apartment which may have been the **Heir's Residence.** It consists of a small hall with pier-and-door partition(63), a court with porticoes on two sides, giving a lovely view of the Lasithi mountains, and a lightwell. Next to it there is a lustral basin (63d) in which libation vessels and models of sacred sym-

Palace of Phaistos. Axial reconstruction (after Hugo-Brunt)

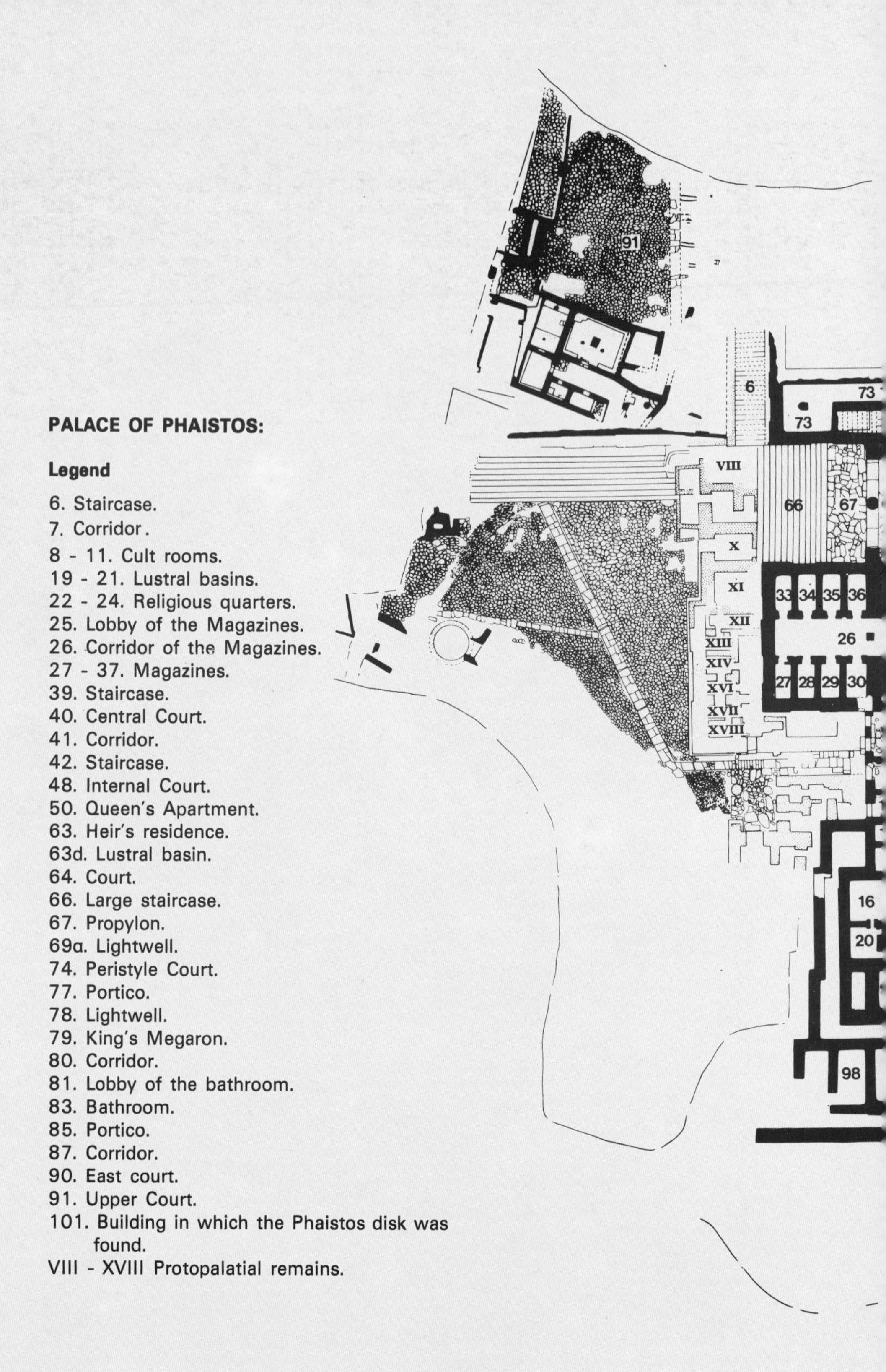

PALACE OF PHAISTOS:

Legend

6. Staircase.
7. Corridor.
8 - 11. Cult rooms.
19 - 21. Lustral basins.
22 - 24. Religious quarters.
25. Lobby of the Magazines.
26. Corridor of the Magazines.
27 - 37. Magazines.
39. Staircase.
40. Central Court.
41. Corridor.
42. Staircase.
48. Internal Court.
50. Queen's Apartment.
63. Heir's residence.
63d. Lustral basin.
64. Court.
66. Large staircase.
67. Propylon.
69α. Lightwell.
74. Peristyle Court.
77. Portico.
78. Lightwell.
79. King's Megaron.
80. Corridor.
81. Lobby of the bathroom.
83. Bathroom.
85. Portico.
87. Corridor.
90. East court.
91. Upper Court.
101. Building in which the Phaistos disk was found.
VIII - XVIII Protopalatial remains.

101
102
103
104
81
82
83
84
85
86
80
79
77
78
93
76
51
50
87
88
89
53
74
48
52
54
56
45
92
91
49
90
55
75
41
46
44
61
69a
58
42
59
60
58
57
43
62
38
39
63
25
64
63 b
a
c
d
e
65
7
40
12
24
13
23
22
96
97
10
0
20M

Palace of Phaistos. Reconstruction of the great propylon (after J.W. Graham)

bols were found.

In the middle of the large **East Court** (90), in the north part of the wing, there is a horseshoe-shaped **bronze-smelting kiln,** on the walls of which layers of smelted metal can be discerned.

North Wing

In this wing the Royal Apartments are located, which is why its facade onto the Central Court was especially splendid. To right and left it was embellished with half colums and alcoves for the royal guard. These «sentry boxes» were decorated with wall-paintings inside. The **corridor** (41) which commences at the entrance had ancillary rooms off both sides and a staircase (42) which led to the upper storey. Here were the formal banqueting halls. The corridor leads into an internal court (48) and another corridor (87) to the west of which are the Royal Apartments. The **Queen's apartment** (50) consists of a luxurious roóm with bench, floor and dado all of gypsum, columned portico and lightwell-court in the centre. It communicates with the **King's apartment** which is north of it and larger. In the main hall (79) there is, as in the royal quarters of the other palaces, a pier-and-door partion. The floor is of white gypsum flags with red plaster in the interstices. The apartment is completed by porticoes on its north and east side (85,77) and a lightwell (78). It is obvious that the architect of the palace selected the location of the Royal Quarters with care and placed

Palace of Phaistos. Reconstruction of the north side of the central court (after J.W. Graham)

them in the north sector for coolness during the summer and an unimpeded view of Mount Ida from the north portico. Further west, a corridor (80) leads to the lobby (81) of the **Royal Bath** (83) which was, at the same time, a lustral basin. The low platform on one side of the bath was to facilitate pouring water from a height over the bather.

Walking up from the Royal Apartments to a higher level, we come to a formal area of the palace, accessible from the West Propylon and the Royal Apartments. It consists of a large court (74) with porticoes on its four sides (reminiscent of a Roman atrium) and part of a hall with pier-and-door partition.

In the **northeast sector,** a group of buildings of the Protopalatial, or more probably, the first phase of the Neopalatial period (101-104). In the first building (101) the famous «Phaistos Disk», a clay disk with hieroglyphic signs stamped on both faces, was found (see Gallery III in the Herakleion Museum).

Corridor of the magazines. →

View of tthe west wing from the «upper» court.

The central court from the SW. Snow-capped Mt. Ida in the background. →

The grand staircase.

The NW side of the central court.

The facade of the north wing, overlooking the central court.

The entrance to the north wing with half columns and niches to right and left.

The King's megaron.

The Queen's megaron.

Inner court of the north wing.

Lobby of the magazines and the NW sector of the central court.

The Theatral area in the West Court and the large staircase of the West Entrance.

VILLA OF AGHIA TRIADA

Excavations here were conducted by the Italian Archaeological School (1902-05 and 1910-11).

This is an opulent Minoan villa in which some exceptional works of art were found, such as the three well-known steatite vases (see Gallery VII in the Herakleion Museum) and wonderful wall-paintings.

It is located at a short distance from the palace of Phaistos, to the west, with which it is connected by a paved road. The view that it was the palace of another overlord who had jurisdiction over the western part of the Mesara plain does not seem very plausible because of the villa's proximity to Phaistos. Perhaps it served as the summer residence of the kings of Phaistos, since it was beside the river with its verdant banks.

The villa was built during the Neopalatial period and destroyed along with the other Minoan centres. In the Postalatial period new buildings were founded upon the ruins of the apartments of the villa (megaron, shrine etc.).

It does not have the typical lay-out of the palaces, nor other villas. There is no central court and it consists of two wings which meet at a right - angle. One is orientated E and the other S.

The **Royal Quarters** are situated at the NW end of the first wing. They consist of a spacious hall with pier-and-door partition (2), portico, lightwell and room with benches (3). The walls were faced with alabaster slabs. A large platform in the next room probably served as a bed. To the north of the pier-and-door partition there is another iuxurious hall with pier-and-door partition (4). It is smaller and must have been the **archive** of the monarch, as is indicated by the numerous sealings (from correspondance) and Linear A tablets which were found there. From an adjacent room to the east came very beautiful wall-paintings. To the south of the large hall with pier-and-door partition there are magazines and servants' quarters.

The central and eastern sector of this wing was occupied by a **Treasury** and **Magazines.** After the destruction of the villa a large **Mycenaean Megaron** was constructed on top of the magazine area and was perhaps the residence of the Mycenaean noble of the region.

On the south side of this wing is the main court of the villa, the **Court of the Altars,** which is also the terminus of the road from Phaistos. To the east of this point there is a **shrine** with benches for figurines and a lavishly decorated floor (see Gallery XIV in the Herakleion Museum) with painted underwater scence. The shrine was built during the Neopalatial period but was also in use during the Postpalatial era.

A large staircase unites the Court of the Altars with the **Ramp** along the length of the north facade of the palace (Rampa dal Mare).

The second wing (orientated N — S) has a large portico of pillars and columns. Eight spacious rooms, surely **shops,** open off this portico on its west side. This unit, which resembles agoras of the Hellenistic and Roman period, has been named the **market place** (Mercato) and is considered to be the oldest «agora» in Greece. On the west side of the wing there are remains of houses from the **settlement** which spread out to the north of the main complex of the villa.

The «Report Cup». Steatite cup with relief representation of a young prince and officer. From the Villa at Aghia Triada.

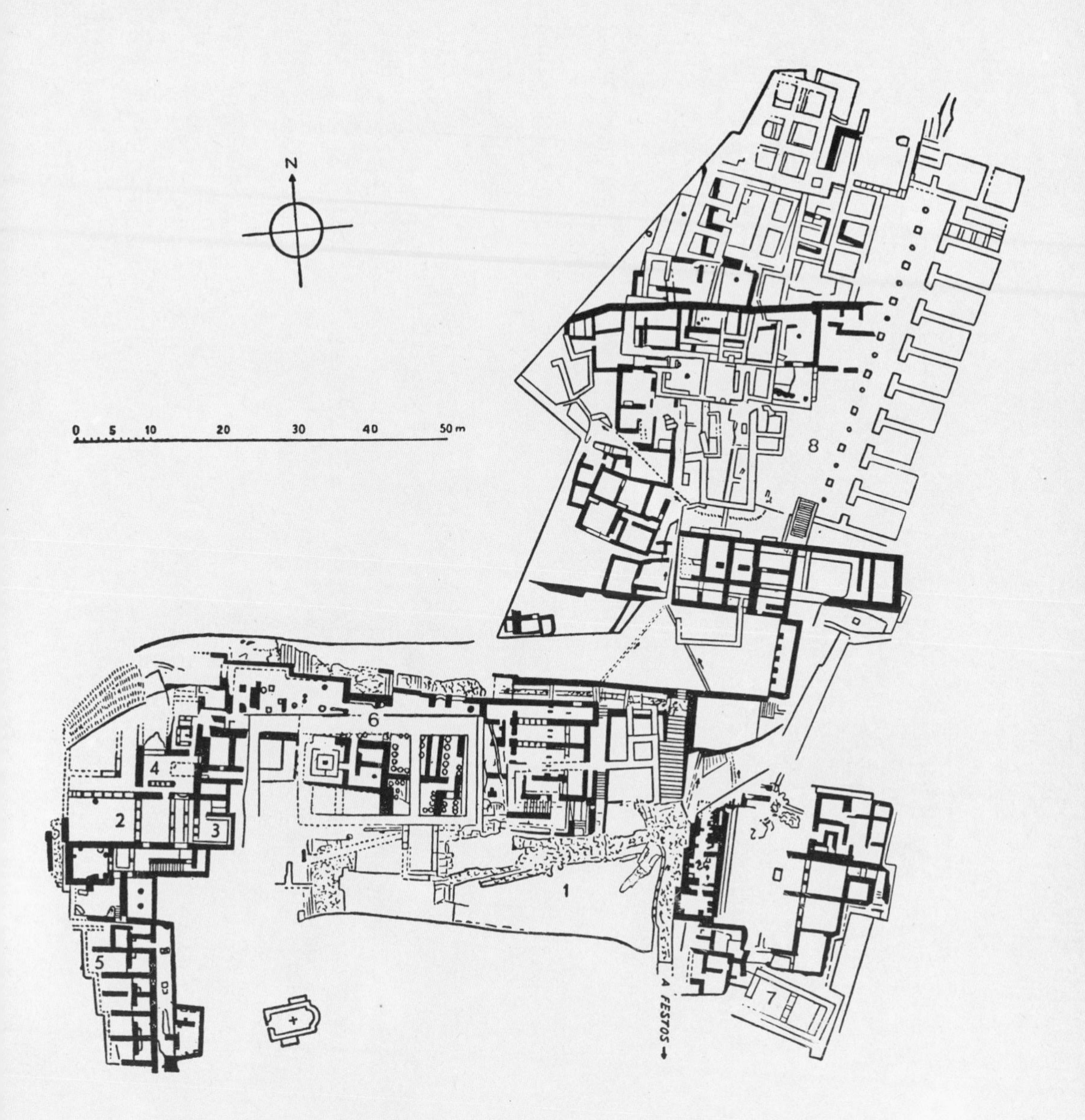

VILLA OF AGHIA TRIADA:

Legend

1. Court of the altars.
2. Pier-and-door partition.
3. Room with benches.
4. Archive.
5. Servants' quarters and magazines.
6. Mycenaean megaron.
7. Shrine.
8. Market place.

Partial view.

Stone water conduits.

Sector of the royal apartments.

The «agora» with stoa and shops.

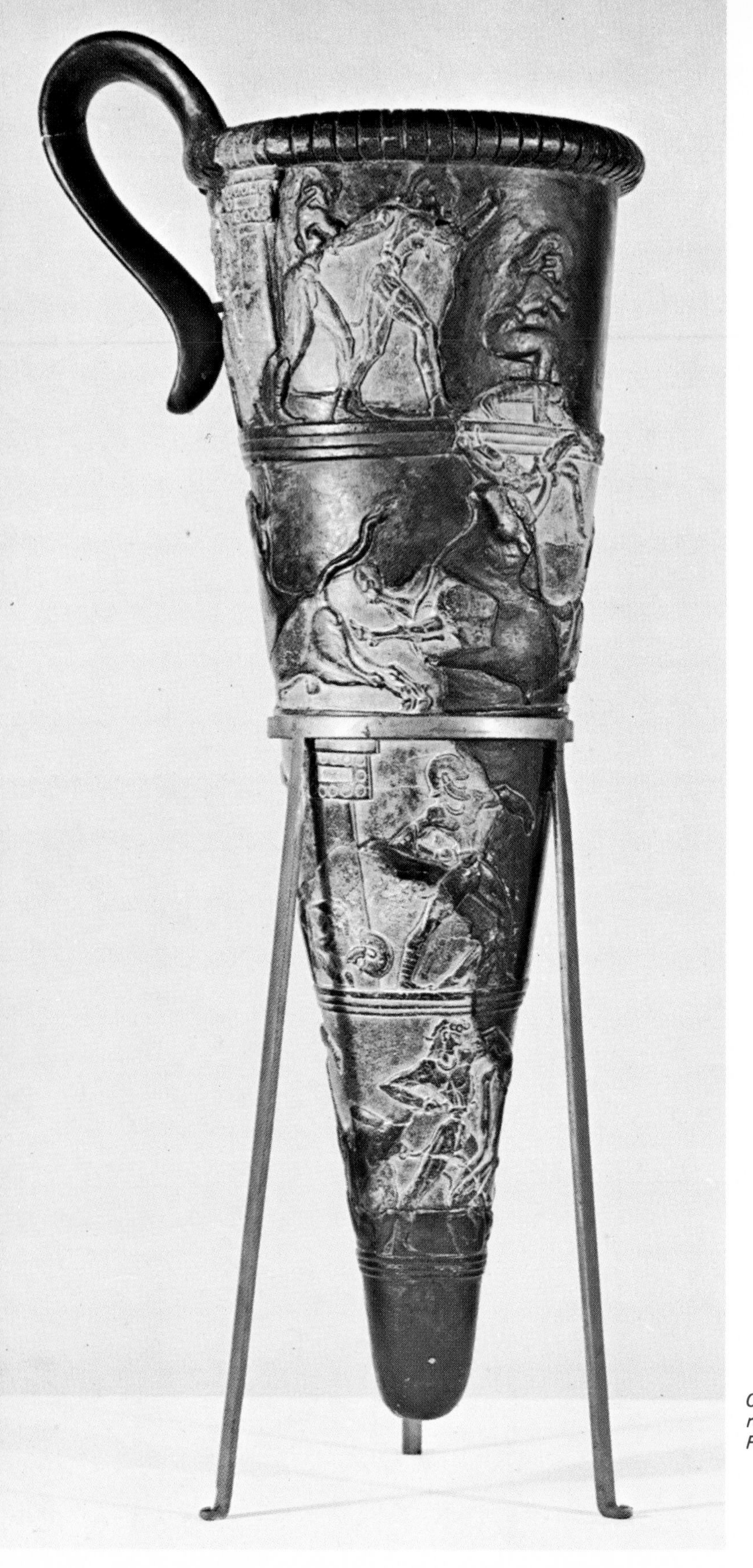

Conical steatite rhyton with relief representations of athletic contests. From the Villa at Aghia Triada.

GORTYN

Gortyn, on the Mesara plain to the NE of Phaistos, was an important ancient city. It formerly occupied a far greater area, extending between the present-day villages of Aghioi Deka and Metropolis. At the time of its acme the city had two harbours on the Libyan Sea, Lebena (present-day Lenta) and Matala which came into its possession when it destroyed and dominated neighbouring Phaistos in the 3rd century BC.

In mythology Gortyn is connected with the famous myth of Zeus and Europe. According to tradition, Zeus, disguised as a bull, abducted Europe, daughter of Agenor, king of Phoinicia, and brought her to Gortyn. There, beneath a plane tree beside the river Lethaios, the union of the god with Europe took place and from this were born Minos, Sarpedon and Rhadhamanthys. It is interesting that most of the coins minted by ancient Gortyn bore the picture of Europe seated on the back of a bull - Zeus -, or Europe seated between the branches of the plane tree.

Indicative of the city's renown is the fact that the great philosopher Plato, in his «Laws», mentions it as a city which prospered and was well - governed. That it had good legislation is also evident from the content of the Great Inscription, of which more will be said below.

As was the case in the other large cities of Crete in historical times, Gortyn's history is full of wars with its neighbours, especially Knossos.

When the Romans intervened in Crete (69 BC) the Gortynians sided with them and thus escaped the fate of other cities, which was complete annihilation. On the contrary, Gortyn became the capital of Crete and Cyrenaica and in Roman times reached its developmental peak. It was the most important city in Crete, with splendid public buildings embellished with a host of statues.

Gortyn was the first city in Crete to accept Christianity and the Apostle Titus was appointed as its first Bishop by St. Paul. One of the earliest churches on the island was built here, the church of Aghios Titus, in the 6th century (see below). The city's floruit continued through into Byzantine times, until 824 when it was totally sacked by the Saracens who dominated Crete.

Monuments:

The ruins of ancient Gortyn, which are nowadays spread over a wide area, were brought to light in excavations of the Italian Archaeological School which were begun during the last century (1884) under F. Halbherr and were continued on a large scale later. The most important monuments revealed are: a temple and a rich votive deposit on the **acropolis** of the ancient city, the **Praetorium,** seat of the Governor of Crete and Cyrene and centre of political life of the Greco-Roman period, the temple of **Pythios Apollo,** the most important temple within which there was an enormous statue of Apollo which is exhibited in the Herakleion museum (Gallery XX), the **Temple of the Egyptian Deities** (Isis, Sarapis), two **Nymphaia,** monumental fountains dedicated to the nymphs, two **theatres** and an **amphitheatre, odeum, forum,** public **baths, stadium** et al.

The Odeum and the Great Inscription

Of the various monuments of the Greco-Roman period the only one which one may easily visit nowadays is the **Odeum.** It was built in the 1st century AD on the site of an earlier building and then rebuilt, after its destruction, in the 3rd century. It has the typical form of a Roman odeum. There were niches for statues in front of the stage and the orchestra was paved with black and white flagstones. The tiers of marble seats are quite well-preserved. The building has two entrances from the north side. On this side, in a sector which is nowadays roofed, the famous **Gortyn Code** is housed. This inscription had originally been written on a circular building which stood in the ancient agora of Gortyn, so that all citizens could read it and learn the laws. Later, in the Roman period, (1st century AD), the stones bearing the inscription were removed from the old, probably destroyed, building and incorporated in the odeum, a much-frequented place, where it was exhibited as a historical heirloom.

Church of Aghios Titus

The inscription is the largest ancient Greek inscription to have survived and is the most significant legal text of Greek antiquity. Indeed, it is considered to be the first European codex of statutes. It has rightly been called the «Queen of Inscriptions» and is dated to circa 500 BC, though it is believed to include decrees of earlier customary law with minor modifications. The inscription is a mine of information about the life and customs of Doric Crete as well as of Cretan jurisprudence which was renowned in antiquity and seems to have influenced the legislation of other ancient cities.

The section of the inscription which is preserved is incised in twelve columns, which is why the text is named «Dodekadeltos». Each column has 53 - 56 lines, so the total number of lines is about 640. The inscription is written in the Archaic Cretan alphabet which had 18 letters instead of 24, as in the typical Greek alphabet. It is written according to the «boustrephedon» system (literally, as the ox ploughs) i.e. from right to left on one line, from left to right on the next et seq.

The inscription is not, of course, a systematic compilation of all regulations of Civil Law, nor is there any sequence in the transition from one topic to another.

The Odeum. At the back Wall of the covered stoa stands the famous inscription with the Laws of Gortyn.

The Temple of Pythios Apollo.

The altar in front of the Temple of Pythios Apollo.

The principal subjects dealt with are: Legal regulation of the personal status of a freeman or slave - Rape and adultery - Adoption - Property relations of spouses - Divorce - Birth of children after divorce - Bequests - Inheritances et al.

Of course the spirit of the Laws is, quite naturally, conservative since at Gortyn, as in the other Doric cities of Crete, the body politic was the oligarchy. However, in many of its decrees the legislation of Gortyn was somewhat progressive as, e.g., in its statutes concerning women's rights and the treatment of slaves. Also of interest is the fact that it lays down a detailed procedure for establishing the objective truth (oath-swearing, more than one witness) and that it forbids illegal detention and taking the law into one's hands.

Aghios Titus

As soon as one arrives at the archaeological site of Gortyn one sees evidence of its Byzantine past, the impressive ruins of a large church dedicated to the first Christian bishop of Crete, Aghios Titus. The church was built in the 6th century and was in use as the metropolitan church of Gortyn, the capital of Crete until the beginning of the 9th, when it was destroyed by the Saracens.

The church has the plan of a three-aisled cruciform basilica with dome. It was roofed with two vaults which crossed (part of the east one is preserved) and a dome, at the point of their intersection. The semicircular apse of the Hieron has survived. Like the smaller apses to right and left of it (prothesis and diakonikon) it was three-sided internally. The large windows in the apses are particularly impressive, as is the lovely isodomic masonry. Generally, it is a magnificent yet very plain building.

PALACE OF MALIA

It is located on the Malia plain on the route to Eastern Crete. It is built on more-or-less flat terrain, very close to the north shore. The ancient name of the region is not known, but it has been maintained that it was most probably Milatos.

First investigations were made by Joseph Chatzidakis in 1915. Shortly afterwards, however, excavations were started by the French Archaeological School, which continues them even today in the surrounding region where a significant part of the city has also been unearthed.

The palace we see today is that which was built in the Neopalatial period (circa 1700 BC) to replace the first palace of the Protopalatial period. This new palace was destroyed in 1450 BC in the general destruction of the Minoan palaces and cities.

The palace is a relatively plain building, constructed of rather poorer materials (limestone, poros sandstone, bricks) and without any use of luxurious gypsum. It occupies an area almost the same as the palace of Phaistos and its lay-out is analogous with that of the other palaces. That is, it consists of four wings built around a central Court, orientated in a N-S direction.

West Wing

The visit begins from the **West Court** which is paved and traversed by a raised «processional causeway» almost parallel with the palace facade. A fork of the causeway leads to the SW corner of the court, where there are the remains of eight **circular buildings** most probably **granaries.** Passing through an opening in the west facade, we find ourselves in a long narrow corridor with **rows of Magazines** on both sides. The east sector of the wing is occupied by the religious quarters. First is an ancillary room where the king prepared himself for official ceremonial appearances. It was here that a large ceremonial sword with rock crystal hilt and a stone mace head in the form of a leopard and axe were found. We then mount a small staircase to the south and come to the main religious room which the excavators called the **«loggia»** i.e. verandah with columns. It is a roofed area which is connected to the Central Court by a wide staircase with a few treads and a column in the middle. The ceremonies held here could be watched by the crowd gathered in the Central Court, since the area is open towards the court and at a slightly higher level.

On leaving the Central Court we see, next to the Loggia, a large **staircase** which led to the upper floor. Further south there is a spacious paved **lobby** with bench, perhaps an audience chamber and **crypt** for sacred rites with two pillars on which are incised symbols of stars, double axes and tridents. A little further down, in the SW corner of the Central Court, we meet a wide staircase which perhaps constitutes the **Theatral Area** of the palace. Next to it is the famous **kernos,** a stone vessel with 34 small hollows around its periphery. In these depressions were placed either assorted fruits, thanksgiving offerings to the deity after the harvest, or seeds, to be

Palace of Malia. Reconstruction (after J.W. Craham)

blessed by the goddess before sowing. The view that the kernos was a game, a type of roulette, does not seem likely. In the south sector of the wing there is a small **shrine** in which ritual vessels and an altar were discovered.

The West Wing is separated from the south, where the workshops are located, by a wide beautifully paved corridor, which comprised the **South Entrance** of the palace.

Central Court

It is smaller than the Central Court of the palace of Knossos and Phaistos (49 × 22 m). Parts of it are paved but it is not certain whether it was completely covered. In the middle, opposite the pillar crypt, we see the **Underground Altar** of which four supports for the sacrificial eschar are preserved.

East Wing

Along the length of the east side of the Central Court are preserved the remains of a **portico** of pillars and columns, between which there was a railing, perhaps to protect the spectators during the execution of bull-sports in the Central Court. The **row of Magazines** behind this portico was for the storage of oil. The magazines have been roofed, but at present cannot be visited. To the south of the wing is the **Southeast Entrance.**

North Wing

There is a **portico** which was isolated from the Central Court by a wall in this wing too. Behind it there is a **lobby** with single pillar and a large **hypostyle hall** with six pillars. Above these two rooms there must have been, as in the palace of Zakros, formal columned banqueting halls, access to which was via the stairway on the right. A narrow corridor leads from the Central to the **North Semiperistyle Court.** The obliquely orientated structure at the edge of its East Portico is perhaps a **Shrine** which was founded here after 1450 BC. Southwest of the North Court we come into another internal court, known as the **Court of the Keep.** A room with very thick walls, in its south sector, named the «keep» by the excavators, was perhaps the royal treasury which had, however, been looted.

Even further west we meet the **King's Megaron** which consists of a paved hall with pier-and-door partition, porticoes and lightwell. The area in front of its north portico, where ruins of the first palace are nowadays visible, would have been a royal garden. The paved lobby next to the hall with pier-and-door partition may have been the Queen's Megaron. To the south there is a **Lustral Basin.** It was next to this lobby that the «acrobat sword» with gold adornment on its hilt bearing the extraordinary relief representation of an acrobat, was found.

Returning, once again, to the North Court, which is surrounded by Magazines and Workshops, we come out of the **North Gate** of the palace from where the paved road leading to the harbour begins.

The North Entrance to the palace and large storage jars (pithoi).

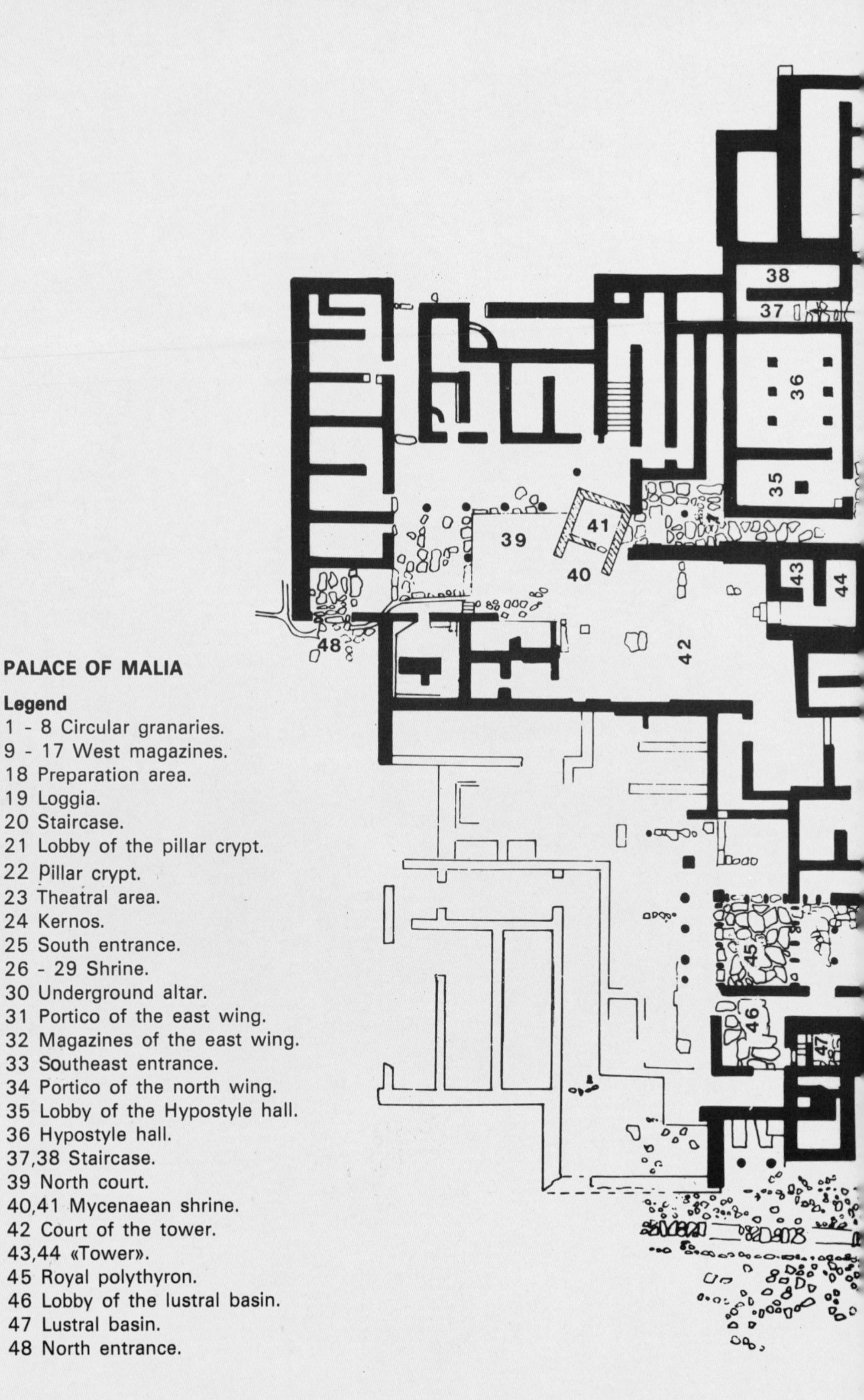

PALACE OF MALIA

Legend
1 - 8 Circular granaries.
9 - 17 West magazines.
18 Preparation area.
19 Loggia.
20 Staircase.
21 Lobby of the pillar crypt.
22 Pillar crypt.
23 Theatral area.
24 Kernos.
25 South entrance.
26 - 29 Shrine.
30 Underground altar.
31 Portico of the east wing.
32 Magazines of the east wing.
33 Southeast entrance.
34 Portico of the north wing.
35 Lobby of the Hypostyle hall.
36 Hypostyle hall.
37,38 Staircase.
39 North court.
40,41 Mycenaean shrine.
42 Court of the tower.
43,44 «Tower».
45 Royal polythyron.
46 Lobby of the lustral basin.
47 Lustral basin.
48 North entrance.

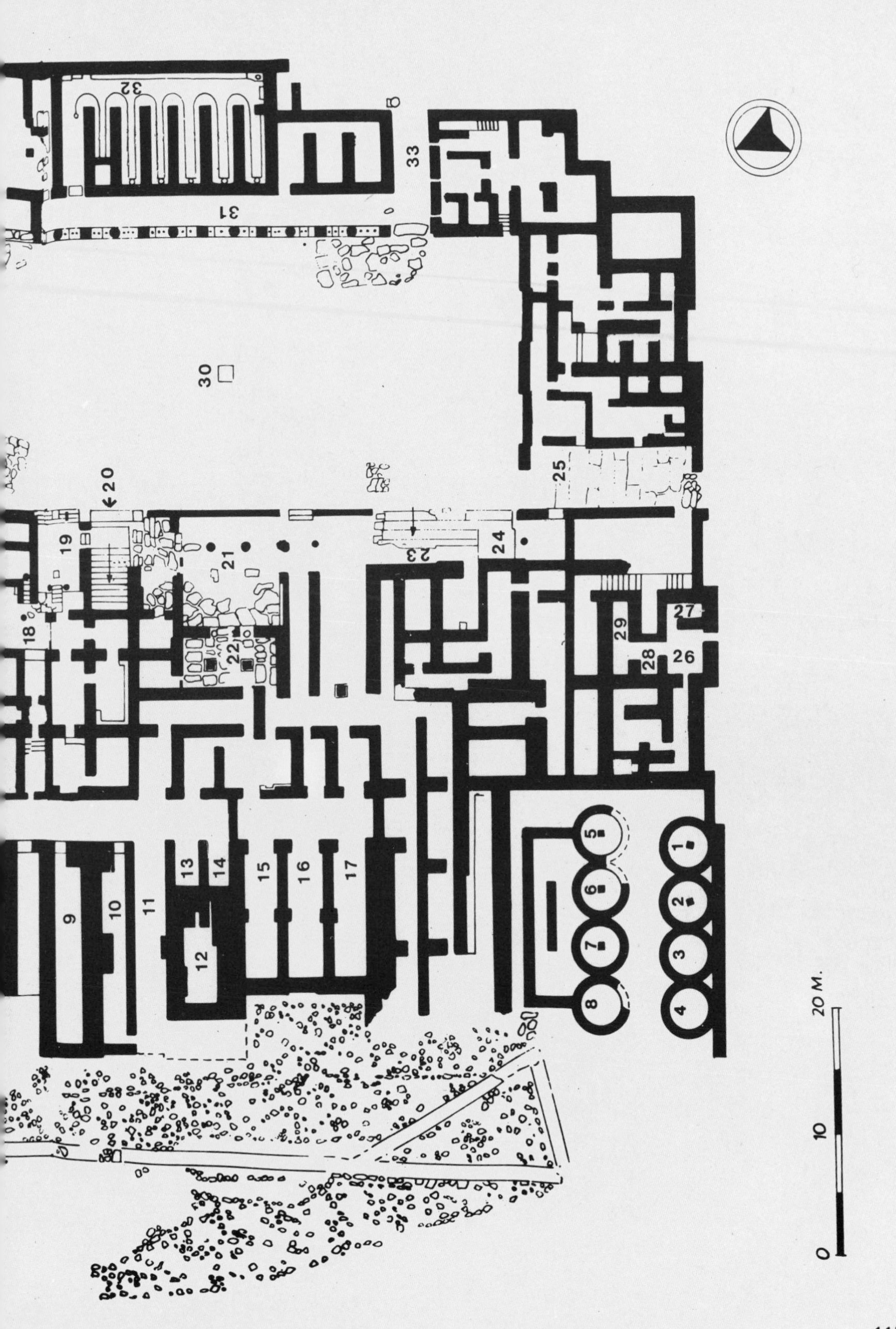

1
2
3
4
5
6
7
8
9
10
11
12
13
14
15
16
17
18
19
20
21
22
23
24
25
26
27
28
29
30
31
32
33
0
10
20 M.

The crypt with the pillars.

View of the central court from the NE.

he famous stone «kernos»,
ssel for offerings to the goddess.

The king's «polythyron».

hypostyle hall of the north wing.

PALACE OF ZAKROS

This is the smallest of the four Minoan palaces, covering an area of 7500 sq. m. It is located at Kato Zakro, Siteia, very close to the sea and seems to have functioned as a base of Knossos, but with autonomous development, for the control of the sea routes in the region of Eastern Crete and trade with Anatolia and Egypt.

The first palace was built during the Protopalatial period and later, in the Neopalatial period, circa 1600 BC, acquired the form we see today. It was destroyed in 1450 BC, perhaps by the eruption of the Thera volcano and the site was not resettled. For this reason it was discovered unlooted with those objects which the inhabitants had left behind when they hurriedly left, shortly before the terrible disaster.

Excavations, conducted by N. Platon, began in 1961 and are still going on in the palace itself and the neighbouring hill with the buildings of the Minoan town.

To enter the palace we follow the oblique paved **road** coming from the harbour. Next to it there are various workshops, including a large **metal-smelting** furnace with crucible, flue etc. The road terminates at the **NE Gate** with the huge monolithic threshold, the main gate of the palace. Descending the stepped ramp from here, we come first to a large paved internal **Court** and, finally, along a corridor, to the Central Court.

Central Court

It is much smaller than the Central Court of the other palaces (30×12 m) and was used, like the others, as a meeting place and for religious rituals. In front of the main door of the West Wing there is a square platform which must have belonged to an **altar.**

West Wing

In it are the religious quarters and magazines. The most important rooms overlook the Central Court. The largest of these is the **Hall of Ceremonies,** a magnificent chamber with interior colonnade, pier-and-door partition and paved lightwell with large windows on the west side. Its floor had unusual decoration with stucco panels. Three doorways connect it with the adjacent **Hall of religious banquets** where many small ewers were found. Its walls and floors were lavishly decorated.

The internal rooms in the western part of the wing are also of a sacred character. Starting at the easternmost, there is a **Lustral Basin** with eight steps, the small **shrine** with bench for the priest and niche for idols and the **Archive** with closets in which Linear A tablets, on which the property of the shrine would have been recorded, were arranged. Further south are the shrine **repositories** and the famous **treasury** with large bin-like containers. This was discovered full of wonderful ritual vessels of polychrome marble, faience et al. (see Gallery VIII in the Herakleion Museum).

In the NW sector of the wing there is a series of **Magazines** in which a considerable quantity of pottery was found.

South Wing

Here there were **Workshops** for the manufacture of objects of precious materials (ivory, rock crystal, faience) and metal.

East Wing

This wing had been extensively destroyed by subsequent cultivation. Thus the lay-out of the Royal Apartments, which were located here, is somewhat difficult to discern. The **Queen's Apartment** with internal pier-and-door partition and lightwell, is the smaller. Next to it is the large **King's Apartment** with pier-and-door partition, portico and lightwell. To the east we see the large **Square Hall** with a **circular cistern** in the centre and traces of the water conduits. The cistern was surrounded by a columned parapet and has a small stairway. It may have been a private swimming pool or aquarium for exotic fish. In any case, many features of the room indicate that it may have been the Throne Room of the palace, where the king received official guests. To the south there is another **sunken spring,** the chamber of which is of extremely careful construction. In the SE corner of the Central Court there is another installation for pumping water. It is a **circular well,** accessible via a staircase, which is built within a rectangular enclosure. Inside this well diverse offerings to the goddess were found, which must have been made shortly before the final catastrophe. Among them was a cup containing olives, wonderfully well-preserved in water. Unfortunately, immediately after they came into contact with the atmosphere they shrivelled.

We now return to the north part of the wing, where a wide corridor links the Queen's apartment with the **Lobby** and **Bathroom** which was at the same time, a **Lustral Basin.** On two of its walls there were raised dais with small columns and niches with a fresco depicting sacral horns upon an altar.

North Wing

It includes a portico with built bench, **Magazines** for comestibles and ancillary rooms full of utilitarian vessels. There is also a large hall with six internal supports which would have served as a **kitchen** and informal dining room. Above the kitchen was the main Royal Banqueting Hall, accessible via a staircase to the east.

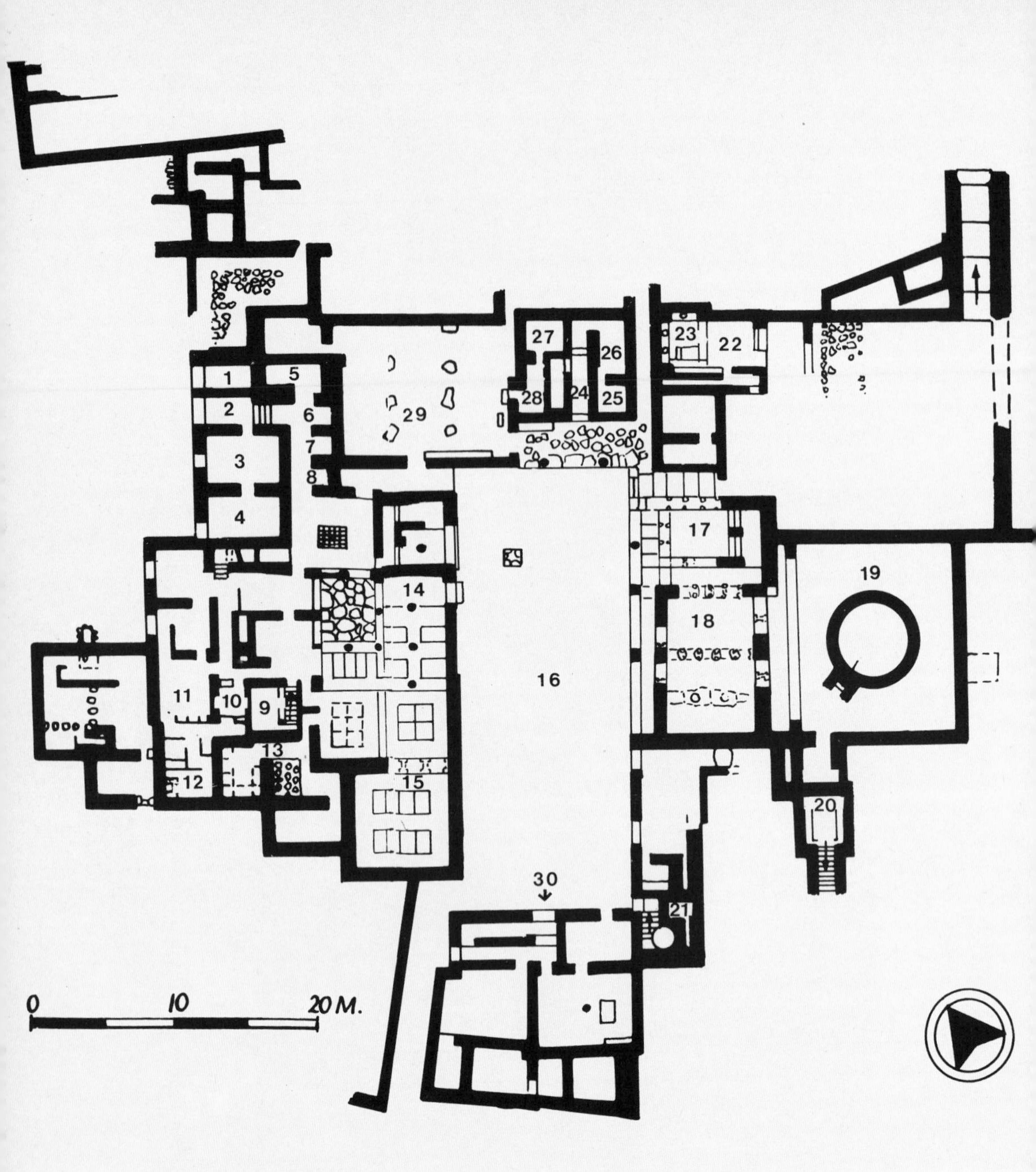

PALACE OF ZAKROS:

Legend

1 - 8 Magazines. 9 Sacred cistern. 10. Shrine. 11 Archive room. 12 Shrine repositories. 13 Treasury. 14 Hall of Ceremonies. 15 Sacred banqueting hall. 16 Central court. 17 Queen's apartment. 18 Kings' apartment. 19 Square hall of the circular cistern. 20 Spring chamber. 21 Circular well. 22 Lobby of the bathroom. 23 Bathroom - Lustral basin. 24 Staircase. 25 - 28 Magazines. 29 Kitchen - dining room. 30 Workshops of the south wing.

The shrine treasury in the West Wing.

Shrine with bench in the West Wing.

The «Hall of Ceremonies» and paved lightwell in the West Wing.

General view. The Central Court in the middle.

The circular cistern in the square room of the East Wing.

Entrance to the West Wing and altar of the Central Court.

GOURNIA

Gournia is a typical Minoan town which came to light at the beginning of the century (1901-04) in the excavations of the American archaeologist Harriet Boyd. It is built on a low hillock beside the sea on the Gulf of Mirabello. In Minoan times its situation was extremely important since it could control the north point of the Isthmus of Hierapetra and the road to Eastern Crete.

This small town has, in addition to the houses and artisans' workshops, a small palace for the local noble and a public shrine. Its floruit is dated to the Neopalatial period, although there are also later ruins. It was destroyed, along with the other Minoan centres, in 1450 BC. Later, in the Postpalatial period, part of the town was reinhabited.

The **houses** are small and built very close together. The majority are two-storeyed and in many cases there is no entrance to the ground floor which seems to have been used as a magazine, accessible via an internal trap-door. The larger rooms would have been in the upper storey.

A rudimentary **street network** existed. The hill is encircled by a peripheral road and another surrounds the eastern quarter, lower down. There are other, intersecting roads, which are frequently stepped where the gradient is steep. All the streets are paved.

There is a **small palace** on the top of the hill, but it is poorly preserved. It was built by the overlord of the town who wished to imitate, on a much lesser scale however, the plan of the large palaces. We can discern a large «public» **court** with the steps of a **«Theatre»,** next to a large flat stone with holes (perhaps used for bull sacrifices), a portico with columns and pillars, long, narrow magazines in the west wing, small West Court in front of the carefully constructed West Facade of the palace et al.

Also of interest is the small **shrine** of the settlement. It is a little room with bench, in which intact ritual vessels were found: clay figurines of the goddess with raised arms, altar, ritual tubular vessels with sacred symbols and snakes et al. (see Gallery X in the Herakleion Museum). These finds are of the Postpalatial period, but the shrine was already in existence in the preceding period.

General view of the settlement.

GOURNIA:
Legend
1. «Public» court
2. Central Hall.
3. Magazines.
4. West court.
5. Shrine.
5
4
3
2
1
10 0 10 20 30

General view of the settlement.

Large stone with holes, perhaps for the sacrifice of a bull.

The Public Court and the Theatre

AGHIOS NIKOLAOS ARCHAEOLOGICAL MUSEUM

Quite a large and important museum containing antiquities from different parts of East Crete.

Of particular interest are the finds from the Prepalatial period of Minoan civilisation, from the settlement of Myrtos and the cemeteries of Mochlos and Aghia Photia: pottery (mottled Vasiliki ware from Myrtos, kernoi and piriform vases from Aghia Photia et al.), primitive potter's wheels, seals, loom weights, obsidian blades, bronze weapons and tools, strange figurine of a goddess with a ewer in her hands (Goddess of Myrtos), lovely stone vases, very fine gold jewellery. Finds exhibited from the other Minoan periods include: votives from the Peak Sanctuaries at Petsopha, Prinia, Zeros et al. (clay figurines of worshippers and animals, stone vases, quadruple sacral horns), pottery from Zakros, Myrsini, Kritsa, Makryyalo et al., bronze weapons (some swords with ivory hilts) and tools, stone communion chalice, jewellery (and a wonderful gold pin with Linear A inscription), seals, **clay** Postpalatial figurine of a worshipper from Myrsini, clay sarcophagi, Postpalatial funerary urn within a small vaulted structure etc.

Composite sacral horns of plaster. Middle Minoan peak sanctuary at Petsophas. *(Photo Hannibal)*

Finds of Historical times: Protogeometric and Geometric pottery from Siteia, many Geometric and Archaic figurines from the deposits at Anavlochos, Siteia and Olounta et al.

Displayed in the last gallery are Roman finds, mainly from Aghios Nikolaos; bronze coins, rings, clay busts et al. The head of a young athlete with his gold wreath still in its original position is a unique find.

CHANIA ARCHAEOLOGICAL MUSEUM

It is housed in the church of St. Francis, which was built during the Venetian occupation of Crete. It contains antiquities of all periods from Western Crete.

Especially interesting is the prehistoric collection. Neolithic vases and weapons. Minoan pottery from Kastelli, Chania (perhaps the palace of Kydonia), Kalami, Chania, the caves of Platyvola and Perivolia, Chania et al. (outstanding are the incised Prepalatial vases from Platyvola and the Postpalatial pottery). Minoan stone vases and bronze weapons. Clay Linear A tablets, polyhedral sealings and disks from Kastelli. Minoan jewellery and sealstones. Postpalatial clay larnakes from the cemetery of Armenoi, Rethymnon with significant painted representations of religious symbols and ceremonies.

The historical collection includes: pottery of all periods, from Protogeometric until Roman. Interesting Archaic figurines from Axos. Hellenistic and Roman figurines. Greek and Roman sculptures. Assorted small objects: alabaster pyxides, weapons, figurines, mirrors, glass vases, jewellery, oil lamps, coins. Mosaic floor with scene of Neptune and the nymph Amymone, from Chania.